Armoured To Find The Light

PASTOR LERONE DINNALL

ISBN 978-1-957582-76-4 (paperback)
ISBN 978-1-957582-74-0 (hardcover)
ISBN 978-1-957582-75-7 (eBook)

Printed in the United States of America

Contents

Targeting...

This Book is aiming to bring forth a specific Message to those who are not yet Saved, for those who believes that they will never become Saved because of their current life's activities, for those who believe that they were born in the wrong family or in the wrong country to satisfy the acceptance of Saving Grace from The Father Above; for those who were taught about the wrong foundation of life. The Lord Is Using this Book to Declare and Decree to Your Soul that He Has Never Lost Sight of You, and all He Needs from those who believes that there is no Hope is the first movement by Faith in the Freewill Direction of Jesus Christ through Repentance, then The Almighty God Will Do The Rest, To Stand Firm In The Covenant Which Manifest That God Is Stronger Than Sin.

For those who are just tired of fixed cycle of life that is not mastered by our own path's direction, but rather, it is structured and cemented in the manifestation of the governance of this sinful and corrupt world, that we are made to be impossible to move out of the fixed system that only has one path, which is down. It can never rise because it has no Eternal Manifestation to allow for its systems and governance to rise and break through to that which seems to be The Impossible.

Introduction

Father, Receive All Glory, Honor and Praise through The Saving Name of Jesus Christ, Amen.

Greetings People of God and especially those who are not yet Saved, accept this introduction in The Wonderful Saving Name of Jesus Christ, The Lamb of God. The Ministry of The Church of Jesus Christ Fellowship in Jamaica presents to the world another Book project inspired by The Living Spirit of God which Moves with Divine Force to establish His Will Being Fulfilled on Earth as it is in Heaven. This Book with the title "Armoured To Find The Light" is Milked from The Hands of God to manifest exactly that which the title of the book suggest, being, to be fully armoured to find God's Light in the lives of people that have not yet identified that the Light of God was already within their vessels, waiting to be activated to perform the mission of Kingdom Values.

Armoured To Find The Light is Book number five from the servant of God Pastor Lerone Dinnall and The Ministry of The Church of Jesus Christ Fellowship. Within this Book it will be observed that the focused is directly linked to those who are Christians, yes, but it will also be identified that there is a strong passion from The Spirit of God to Speak to those His People that have not yet experienced The Divine Touch of The Father Above, those who are potential tithes for the land that must be engrafted in The Ministry of God's Love.

I've identified for myself while growing that God's People are not necessarily those who find themselves being apart of a Ministry, which sees themselves entering a building to manifest the purpose of worship to God, but I've identified through the direction of The Father to see Spiritually and be focused on those people of which their Souls is directly linked to The Father Above without the direct establishment of a Ministry. A Ministry is a Spiritual Aid to assist an individual to find the true path that leads to God, this does not mean that a person's only path to God must follow the direct rule of a Ministry, but rather to follow the direct belief of repentance through the access Name of Jesus Christ, The Lamb that was slain for the reconciliation of man to find their path back to God.

Armoured To Find The Light begins with a beautiful message that will allow people from under the sun to identify the foundation of the value of God, this message will allow us to take a second look at our existence for God to therefore seek to protect at all cost that which is God's Value for our lives and that of our children's future. The Book continues with the second message that will feed the People of God with Spiritual Manner to identify that which will grant access for anyone to grow Spiritually in God and also that which will place Eternal Chains on our feets to bar the People of God from Spiritually growing in God's Approval, and this is identified in the person that allows their souls to become a vessel of honor for the truth of God, and in person that grants access for their souls to become a vessel to dishonor that generates lies.

It is The Revelation of God to me that I've identified that if a Child of God remains in ignorance, then that's the same Child of God that has bought their ticket for the merry go round of life's journey, not being able to identify the sure danger of the life we live, because of the acceptance of the traditions that bears no Spiritual Values. Message number three of this Book will reveal Delicate Spiritual information for the life of every Christian, it is a must know, seeing that The Lord Basically Burned for me to reveal this message for His Children to know what is the direct flow of Spiritual Blessing Continuation. If our Spiritual Blessing Continuation is altered or killed, it's not the fault of our Father, but rather, it is the lack of our spiritual discipline to know how to keep that which God has Given to us through the acceptance of our Clean Sacrifice through His Will being done in our lives.

Message number four will tutor every person who desires to identify a true relationship with their Father. I've expressed from my experience with my God of what it took for me to develop and maintain a connection with God that remains solid, therefore, I believe that a true report from a Son of God that has walked on this pathway will be beneficial for all God's People and for those who are not yet saved to identify what it will take for a person to develop Spiritual Connection with God.

Message number five is a Discipline that not many saints have acquired, but relationship with God Reveals that every discipline that a Child of God can maintain will definitely grant access to Divine Spiritual Growth from The Father Above, thus it is seen that there are Children of God that possess different talents and gifts that was only granted access from Their Father Above, because of the Fixed Discipline that such a Child of God has mastered to fulfill for a daily routine.

Message number six to eight speaks of a Child of God's Soil prepared to receive that which God has Given, message number nine is a guideline for every Child of God to know exactly what is God's Expectation for a life with their Father that will keep The Covenant of Peace unbroken. Message number ten will change people's lives, especially those who are at a crossroad that is leading to their own destruction in hell. This message will grant Spiritual Assurance for every believer to identify that God's Hands is filled with Divine Purpose for our lives, even if we have not seen it for ourselves.

The eleventh Chapter of this Book will demonstrate to all people the danger of lust, it will also express that lust is so destructive that it needs no permission or invitation from another to take effect within the lives of people. Chapter twelve will identify a Child of God's True Friend, a lot of imposters are always lurking but a true friend from God is always fixed.

Chapter thirteen is a warning for God's People, it's not a story or something that is made up, but rather it's a true life's event, it happened, and it was not pleasant, it hurts and it still leaves a scar, therefore, for those who will read this message and learn from my mistakes, you'll find yourself in a better position to build a life for your families without the hidden secrets of the fine prints. It's a Warning!

To ask someone to wait is not easy, especially when that person is fueled and fixed to receive that which they desire to receive, unless a person at times feels for themselves, they will never become knowledgeable to accept the discipline of just waiting on God's

Timing, Chapter fourteen will no doubt solidify a Child of God's Faith to just rest in God and wait for God's Divine Movement.

Danger! Danger! Danger! A statement and warning like this to a Child of God would be good whenever it is that they are to be exposed to that which will create damage for themselves and for their family and circle, but this is not always the case. Many things that is granted the approval to destroy a Child of God is that which is spiritually hidden and creeps, therefore, if a Child of God is not Spiritually Connected to their Father, the warning signs of Danger Ahead will definitely be missed, therefore, that Child of God will find themselves suffering the sure consequences of those things that will alter the relationship of how a Child of God have made themselves to become discipline to serve their Father. Message number Fifteen will grant Spiritual Guidance for a Child of God to be able to Identify all the warning signs of destruction that are fixed to break down, steal, kill, and destroy everything that The Father has furnished for a Child of God to have freely. This Message is also a Warning!

Chapter Sixteen and Seventeen are for the Children of God who consider themselves to be men of valor that the Bible spoke about.

These men were the mighty men, they were the professionals in their area of war, these two chapters are speaking however of a spiritual war and not a physical war that can be seen and be dismantled with physical strength. There are times we the People of God just don't know how to fight a spiritual war, through experience and Divine Revelation from God, The Lord Taught me, so that I can Teach His People some simple but Spiritually Effective Disciplines to observe to know how to not only stop spiritual attacks, but also to know how to redirect that which has been granted the spiritual weapon to destroy everything that a Child of God has received from their Father's Hand. Let me put this simple; any Child of God that does not know how to fight the spiritual dark war is a dead Child of God, everything that God has Granted the access for that Child of God to have will be taken away by spiritual assigned demons. The Bible says that the thief cometh not but to steal, kill and to destroy. This passage of Scripture is speaking about a spiritually fueled demon that has been given their assignment to destroy a targeted Child of God's life.

The finale of this Wonderful, Spiritual Educated Book will place the People of God on The Spiritual Double Watch to ensure that, that which is our Birthright from our Father will always remain with us and our children for all existence because we have not learnt the lesson only for ourselves, but also for our children to know what it will take for them to also keep that which God has Granted for their existence to have The Heavenly Eternal Approval to command upon their lives and the lives of their children to follow.

This Book with the title Armoured To Find The Light has been Approved by The Living Eternal Spirit of The Father to break the chains from the lives of those who were held captive for so long, to now begin the journey of a life within The Light of God. Let those who have read this Book, observe with an open eye that God is Gathering His People in one belief to know that His Coming is so near, therefore, we must find ourselves not getting ready like the five foolish virgins but be ready like the five wise virgins. I Pray that The

Father of All Authorities Will Spread His Word to The Tithes of the land, God Bless you, in The Saving Name of Jesus Christ, Amen.

Opening Scriptures

Genesis Chapter 1:1-5.

"In the beginning God Created the Heaven and the Earth. And the Earth was without form, and void; and darkness was upon the face of the deep. And The Spirit of God Moved upon the face of the waters. And God Said, Let there be Light: and there was Light. And God Saw the Light, that it was good: and God Divided the Light from the darkness. And God Called the Light Day, and the darkness He Called Night. And the evening and the morning were the first day".

St John Chapter 1:1-5.

"In the beginning was The Word, and The Word was with God, and The Word was God. The same was in the beginning with God. All things were made by Him; and without Him was not anything made that was made. In Him was life; and the life was the Light of men. And the Light Shineth in darkness; and the darkness comprehended it not."

Mindset

- If something isn't real, why pursue it; If something is REAL, why not pursue it with all your Mind, Heart and Soul.
- To Distinguish Real is to identify that which is FIXED and last for ETERNITY, which means that it has no diluting, meaning that it's not a phase or a season that passess us by for us to relive that season for a next year and hope that the drive which was received from the first experience will be the same or better for the next experience of that season which is to come.
- Look in the mirror and observe yourself to identify that life cannot be just a circle, why a circle when it is that there is the revelation of growth within a person, within an animal and within the plants of this world.
- Is everything already Fixed to pattern our motion to that which the governance of our circle so dictates for it to be, or is there really an Eternal Hope which can be born into, to thus achieve A Divine Spiritual Encounter.
- If we identify that bad things really exist, then how is that we are so blinded to appreciate and accept that good things are real and even strengthened to even greater good things through the Manifestation of The Father Above.
- How deep can darkness become, should we seek to find out?

- How bright can light be, should we stay away from it?
- How deep is God's Mercy?
- How High is God's Love for us?
- How Mysterious and completely out of our hands the Future is, but for our Father, there is no puzzle, He Knows the entire Table of our lives combined.
- Prolonged Darkness is never good because it feeds to establish a wider dimension of its manifestation.
- The Beauty about a prayer to our Father is that it can be done in the darkness, it can be completed in a whisper, it can be mused in the spirituality of our mind without anyone knowing that a prayer to The Almighty God was just established.
- Darkness without God's Manifestation or Permit is completely dangerous, not half but fully dangerous, because there is no direction, whether physical direction or Spiritual Direction, it does not exist, because darkness is what it is, just being dark.
- When The Call from darkness is activated by our Father, remember to do everything within your power to move, even when moving seems impossible, just move, because if you weren't important to our Father then you could not hear The Cry of Light in the darkness that you've now become.
- Observe to understand, darkness never has a future, it has promises that will never be fulfilled, therefore, whenever a person hears The Divine Call of God through their own personal experience that you know is real and not something that someone has manipulated, but it's coming from God with The Eternal Evidence of God's Grace, then this person must understand very quickly to accept The Invitation of God's Light before The Call of Light from Our Father has Moved, because The Invitation to Light

will never remain forever, it has a season for its Release from God and has a season to find a replacement for The Invitation of Light that was offered to the original vessel.

- God Only Makes The Call to Light because He Sees that the person who is in darkness, their time is up, the journey has now reached a crossroad, it's either this person will accept The Call to God's Light or they will remain in darkness that eventually will swallow the last remaining light of that person's existence.

- Yes, there is still hope, Yes, there is still Salvation, The Father of The Entire Universe Declares and Decrees that there is still hope for those who are covered by darkness who has kept a small hope of light still burning deep down inside the Soul where the darkness can never touch.

- God Sees the small light because He Is and Always Was and will Always Be The Greater Light to Shine to thus make The Divine Connection to those who believe that their hope is buried.

- There is no Darkness thicker than Life, Death and Hell, and Our Father Conquered all through the Sacrifice of Jesus Christ, He Declares that He has The Keys of Hell and of Death.

- No matter how thick the darkness of our life becomes, once there is still life in us, it means that there is still hope for us from God if we are securing the small light, and have a great desire to change from darkness to God's Light.

- How do you know that God Is Real and is Speaking Directly to you, start to develop something real for God in secret, Speak to our Father through The Access Name of Jesus Christ, really seek God's Face, enter in some meaningful discipline with God, try to establish at least one day of clean fasting within a month, at least for a few hours for that one day, read The Holy Bible, take 10% of the day to meditate on God, then you'll discover for yourself that Relationship has been Birth, and God will then Speak to that person who is now in Relationship with Him, and you'll identify for yourself without anyone's interference that God Is God and was always waiting on ME.

- God has always been Interested in the few that will believe in Him; Are you one of The Chosen Few?
- Believe In The Saving Name of Jesus Christ, it will surprise you to see for yourself of The Almighty Power that this Name Is Armoured With, To Break Impossible Chains from the Lives of those who are Chosen and Fixed for Light Manifestation in God's Kingdom.

A World Without God...

Message # 164   **Date Started November 17, 2020**
Date Finalized November 17, 2020.

Greetings in The All Powerful Name of Jesus Christ, The Name through which every knee must bow and all tongues will confess that He Is Lord. Happy to find myself again in this purposeful position of Heaven's Value to be of some assistance to the lives of those that need to feed their souls with the continual belief that there is in fact A True and Living God that Sits High and Looks low.

I've intentionally presented the title of this Message in an incline format just to bring across the point that is to be made in this Message.

Adam and then Eve were Created by God to Stand Upright before God, meaning that there was no mediator between The Almighty God and Adam along with his wife Eve, the moment Adam and Eve disobeyed God's Direct Order they surrendered their position of Uprightness with God thus they and their entire generation was not able to stand again in that Position of Uprightness to have direct Access to The Almighty God, it was always the manifestation from that act of disobedience for God to have a mediator at all times to bring forth Divine Communication from God to mankind and never direct access of the position of Uprightness with God.

From The Dispensation of Innocence to now Saving Grace the Position of Uprightness for man to God is always the seeking, some men of old and present have reached to some type of standard of Uprightness with God seeking to gain again that rightful Position but the truth is, that Divine Upright Position with God will only be partly released to mankind because of the law of the flesh, even though we would seek to again entertain that Exclusive Position of Uprightness, it remains within the balance of time and space to now seek to gain just a fraction of The Pure Glory that Adam and Eve did receive from God.

This doesn't mean that those of us who are Christians should just surrender our hope in God for that Divine Experience of Upright Position, No, Full Glory of Uprightness will never be achieved in the law of the physical but every man's piece of Relationship experience is certainly available for that man's personal walk with their Father to know that when this life is over and the law of the physical has ran it's full course, then The Law of The Spiritual begins for all those who have started their own personal path of Uprightness back to The Will of The Father that must start in the law of the physical.

Has I've identified that the title of this message is done in an incline format, just image asking any builder to construct a home or a place of employment or any building in the format that the foundation of the building has an 90 degree difference from where the roof of that building is finalized without any beams, columns or cables to support the incline design of that building. I know some builders would agree that this type of work is possible because we're still living in a world where ignorance is more evident than pure knowledge. But to suggest this idea to a professional Architect and Builder because of The Spirit of Excellence within that Builder he would then understand that the spirits of those ideas to construct a building in that format is completely a different spirit's flow from that which has made him to be excellent in that which he now has a reputation to protect for himself and continual legacy. Something is either possible or it doesn't make sense to do it.

A World Without God, can you believe that we're doing a Topic like this?_____. But if it wasn't necessary The Lord would not awaken me from sleep to do a Message like this. The time currently is 4:12 am, that means I began this message about 3:30 am. Just allowing my readers to know what God Does within me, when everyone is sleeping and enjoying rest, I'm asked to write messages and give them away to those who will accept A Word from The Lord, Yes, I know that not all will believe but what about the few that will believe, and I think that's the Focus of our Father to Reach The Sure 10% of people that are His Tithes for the land.

I took the liberty to look for the meaning of the word Anarchy and this is what it states:

Anarchy:- "A state of disorder due to absence or non-recognition of authority or other controlling systems, lawlessness".

Now this type of condition is not desirable by any I should think but if the ways of a man leads that man away from The Way of God then it is common understanding to know that any path that moves away from the only path of life can never lead to good.

Currently there are many efforts being implemented by the world at present to just erase the thoughts and the mention of God from everything. What will the world look like without God?_.

"God's Value to Mankind"...

- God Is the very Air that we breathe.......
- God Is the Love that we experience.......
- God Is the Family that we never knew we could receive.......
- God Is seen in the Baby that is born.......
- God Is the Health that we enjoy.......
- God Is the Peace that no one can take away no matter what they do......
- God Is the Friend that Visits us in our sleep and tells us that all will be well even when all things look dead.......
- God Is the Sudden Instruction of change when we were well patterned to do that which is customary for us to fulfill.......
- God Is The Voice that Speaks to demons and legions that are set to destroy our lives.......
- God Is The Flow of Positive energy that flows within our lives, for our business and our families.......
- God Is the only Voice that Says Yes when every other voice says no.......
- God Is the only Voice that Says No when every other voice says yes.......
- God Is the Sure Inheritance for an uncertain tomorrow.......
- God Is the Plan that will never fail even when all other plans have already failed.......
- God Is the Mystery above all wisdom.......

- God Is the Access to all life's success, making recommendations for us that we don't even know…….
- God Is The Key and also The Door, it's futile to not have God by your side…….
- God Is The Sense in a Senseless world…….
- God Is the Compassion that is felt in our leader's voice and action to people because they also know that they too need compassion from their Father…….
- God Is the Honesty that makes the moral of people strong that also continues to our children to come…….
- God Is the Fear that people express just to do everything to please God's Will…….
- God Is the Building and Keeping of every city because of the evidence of Righteousness…….
- God Is the Only One to Look down and Say I Forgive…….
- God Is The Living Conscience in every man to do the right thing…….
- God Is The Promises that must be fulfilled because it was Spoken by His Will Being Done…….
- God Is The Invisible Defence for all His Children…….
- God Is The Only Authority…….

Speaking about God and coming into the understanding about who God Is makes a believer look at the world as being small because The God of The Entire Universe is so Big. How does a person even seek to fight A Force that is everywhere and in everything and above all things, how and when if ever?_____.

No one can fight God but they can seek and will always try to stop The Flow of God's Spirit which is reliant on vessels and that's what the forces of the world are seeking to implement their tactics of eliminating the thought of God from the lives of people.

Knowing God starts with a belief that there is A God, that same belief moves on to become Relationship with God.

Therefore, the way in which the world would seek to erase God from the mind of mankind is to erase God's Value step by step, a little at a time until everyone is completely consumed by the new wine to believe that there is no God. This exposure starts with one person then it moves to people, then a community, then a whole parish begins to believe that there is no God, then country, then it will be seen that those countries that are exposed to the bad wine or spirits to believe that there is no God will now seek to influence other countries with their bad medicine, but The People that knows their God shall be strong and do exploits.

I was speaking to The Church the other day just to encourage even myself and this word came out of my mouth from nowhere, and it goes like this:

> **God Is Never Weak, our conditions make it seem like God is weak but if we just look to analyze our situation we would then discover that our condition in that moment of time is so unbearable that we believe that it is God that is weak not knowing that God Is Never Weak!**

How can we ensure that we keep The Flow of God's Spirit Strong for our lives, for our families, for our communities and for our country and even the world?_____.

It begins with the man in the mirror then it must be spread to our circle then communities will be involved, parishes and countries will maintain the strength of The Almighty God, then we'll find ourselves now teaching other countries how to fear and serve The True and Living God because the man in the mirror have made the decision that it must start with me. Even if the opportunity is not there for a person to physically enter into a building to serve The True and Living God, that Relationship must already have been in practice for that man's own discipline, therefore going to Church or not, God's belief remains firm for that man that the world will never be able to take it away.

The world can never take away something that is real, something that an individual has experienced for themselves, and that's what God Must become in the lives of people especially in these times. Say No to the world, you will never take away by belief in God. No, No, No, it's not for sale. No, No, No, I won't trade that which I have for Silver or Gold.

I hope God's People were blessed by these words, again, I direct my readers to The True Source of Inspiration, Jesus Christ, Lord and King, to Him Be All Glory, Honor and Praise from Eternity to Eternity, Amen. From Pastor Lerone Dinnall and The Ministry of The Church of Jesus Christ Fellowship, Savannah Cross, Jamaica, West Indies. God's Mercies Continually.

Just Imagine A World Without God, Think, That's Just Scary, Hell On Earth, Truth!

A Liar, Who Is A Liar?

Message # 151   Date Started August 27, 2020.
                                   Date Finalized August 27, 2020.

Revelation Chapter 22:12-15.

"And, behold, I Come quickly; and My Reward is with Me, to Give every man according as his work shall be. I Am Alpha and Omega, The Beginning and The End, The First and The Last. Blessed are they that do His Commandments, that they may have right to The Tree of Life, and may enter in through The Gates into The City. For without are dogs, and sorcerers, and whoremongers, and murderers, and idolaters, and whosoever loveth and maketh <u>A Lie</u>".

Greetings to The Family of God through The Only Access Name of Jesus Christ our Lord and Savior. As always, All Praise, Glory and Honor be Lifted up to The Only One God which only Has One Mind which leads to only One Direction for His People to enter Heaven.

I just woke up from sleep, the hour is currently 5:35 pm, after sleeping for about two hours because I was so tired having not received my fair share of sleep for the morning which is 8 hours, I got about 4 hours of sleep instead. I heard The Voice of The Lord Speaking to me and also Revealing that I must get up and do a Message about who is A Liar, The Lord Said this Message will forever act as a Guideline for Future generations to be able to conquer the sure spirit of who is A Liar and what not to do to become A Liar and the sure consequences of a person who Is A Liar. Immediately The Appetite for sleep went and I was now Spiritually hungry to get up and make certain to flow with the Inspiration of The Spirit of God that just Spoke to me to fulfill a task for Heaven.

I've already mention in about two Messages that I wrote some details about A Liar, therefore, I never really saw the importance of doing a Message about A Liar seeing that there is already some knowledge of this spirit to be found in what I have already written, but when The Spirit of God Moves to Inspire Heaven's Value that must be practiced on Earth's Training Ground, A Child of God with Purpose has to align himself to that which is The Full Direction of The Spirit of God's Flow.

It is the full understanding of God's People currently to identify that everything that leads to a person committing a sin is as a result of a spirit direction that moves through that person to allow for them to sin. It's not the fault of the spirits that are in the atmosphere but rather it is the Free Will of the vessel which allows for those spirits to have a sure home for their continual manifestation. A person who commits or performs A Lie, this is a movement of a spirit's direction that flows through the fixed spiritual level of condemnation. What this means as The Lord Revealed to my understanding is that a person who is overcomed by a spirit of A Lie by their own Free Will of accepting that spirit is the same person that has to remain under the spiritual rule of that spirit to continue and forever to speak and to maintain that Lie for all Existence of their vessel.

This person or vessel that has freely accepted the spirit's flow to Lie is now spiritually bound by Invisible Chains that shackles their entire vessel from Spiritual Movement towards any manifestation of

Spiritual Growth from God. This means that this person or vessel is Spiritual Stuck and this Spiritual Prison of Chains can only be broken if this person or vessel have now come to themselves to understand that the power to break Spiritual Chains is found in themselves to Repent which will then activate Clean Spiritual Movement from God which will identify that this person or vessel will confess to themselves first, then confesses to God The Commander and Chief of All Spiritual Laws, then this same person must find themselves confessing to those who they have told the Lie to and most important, those who they have told the Lie on. Without this type of Spiritual Direction of Truth from this vessel or person, this person or vessel will remain in a Spiritual Prison Activated by The Order of God's Spiritual Laws to remain in that Spiritual Prison locked away from Spiritual Growth.

A Liar, Who Is A Liar?_____. A Liar can be the person that we see when we look in the Mirror, A Liar can be everyone that we come in contact with, A Liar can be our own mother and father, A Liar can be our Pastor or a Minister of Religion. The main thing to identify through this Topic is to understand that A Liar is any One or any System or Rule or Governance, in other words, People, Places and all Things that moves in the direction to tell A Lie or Make A Lie or Maintain A Lie, this same Person, People, Places and Things is in violation of God's Spiritual Law for Growth and Mercy and Development, Success, Favors, and most important God's Order.

It is important to point out in this Message that if a person is not aware of what is The Truth then that person have not really told A Lie, therefore, it is identify that all those who would seek to give advice that leads to sure direction of people's lives, these are the same people that must make certain that they already know for sure what are the Facts, The Truth. If this person is aware of all the Facts and Truth and then seeks to hide that Truth and make A Lie from that Truth, which will see the Direction of People, Places and Things now move in The Direction which is A Lie, then that same person is the sure vessel which has told A Lie and will manifest and continue to maintain that which is A Lie.

A Person that gives advice based on other people's recommendations, if the recommendation from others is A Lie then that person who has received the recommendation of A Lie and also manifest that which was recommended has also indirectly told A Lie based on the Lie that they have been programmed with. It is identified that a person must always be certain of the source of their Facts, it comes back to a person's circle, exactly that which is a person's circle must also establish and manifest a person's foundation. If a person's circle is A Lie, then that same person's manifestation **MUST** establish their **FOUNDATION**.

Let me give a Testimony: A few years ago something took place at The Church I attended first, this being my Grandfather's Church, that which took place called for a meeting with the Officers of The Church, and within the meeting we needed to establish why what took place actually happened. I spoke in the meeting and explained what I saw took place to the best of my understanding, a Missionary got up after and explained, that what I explained, that was not the way it happened and she gave her version of what happened that called for this meeting's discussion. At the end it was unclear what really happened because there were a lot of different stories from others that lead in different directions, and that's what the spirit of A Lie does.

If Truth is not being manifested in anything that a person seeks to fulfill, then all the other directions of spirits will now take root in whatever we will now seek to manifest!

At the end of the meeting the Missionary came to me and confessed that what she said in the meeting was not true but she had to tell A Lie because she was embarrassed. I looked at her and said that this doesn't mean anything to me because all those who heard you in the meeting believed that you were speaking the Truth and I was speaking A Lie, so how does your apology help me if everyone is still thinking and have accepted that I have told them A Lie?

I hope someone has learnt something from that Testimony. It is still A Lie if there is at least one person that still believes that what you have told them was the Truth. There is a saying that goes like this:

"Words Are Like The Wind".

The Lord would have me to know that every word that a man will speak must be placed on The Measuring Scale of The Almighty God. The Lord Revealed to me that it is best for A Child of God to speak less, and only speak when it is that you are required to speak, and when A Child of God speaks, we must make certain at all times that we are found on The True Foundation of God, because words spoken is not wind, they are formed to bring forth a sure manifestation whether it be good or evil, once it is spoken by a vessel it must be Spiritually Measured by God to bring forth the sure Rewards of that which was manifested by us.

Here is a secret that The Lord Revealed to me, The Lord Views Three Manifestations at all times, The Past, The Present and The Future, therefore, A Child of God must be at all times Patient to move especially when you're not certain of the environment and spiritual governance. I believe this secret however is tied up in The Holy Ghost, this is it: Whatever A Child of God is doing, it must be carefully measured with the consciousness of Past, Present and Future. What this means is that at all times this same Child of God must be Spiritually Focused to SEE exactly what is the spiritual movements of spirits and also The Spiritual Movement of Spirit. They are both different and lead in different directions at all times, not sometimes but all the time.

When A Child of God has Learned and has mastered their own direction's wave, then that same Child of God can enter and be placed in any environment governed by spirits and also be able to conquer their own direction's wave within that environment and also the direction's wave of that same environment.

A Child of God Direction's Wave within their own environment will not have the same pressure points when it is now placed in another environment governed by spirits.

When I tell The People of God that God Is Excellent, now you can see why I say that! Every Direction From The Spirit of God is Aligned with The Sure Manifestation of The Three Views of God Being Past, Present and Future in accordance to God's Will Being Done. If A Child of God is placed in an environment governed by spirits and has not learned The Spiritual Eye, then that Child of God will Adopt and receive the environment's spirits that will manifest that this Child of God will not only tell Lies but continue to speak, manifest and maintain those Lies. **YOU'VE BEEN WARNED!**

Unto The Excellent Father Be All Glory, Honor and Praise through The Access Name of Jesus Christ, Amen. From Pastor Lerone Dinnall and The Ministry of The Church of Jesus Christ Fellowship, Savannah Cross, May Pen, Clarendon, Jamaica, West Indies. God's Continual Guidance and Blessing.

Don't Become A Liar, Speak The Truth And Continue To Be The Truth!

It Is The Spiritual Requirement Of God To Release A Blessing Through The Vessel Of Someone That Is Already Blessed By God.

Message # 92
          Date Started March 4, 2018
Date Finalized March 10, 2018.

To God Be All The Glory, The Honour and Praise; I Greet all God's Children in The Wonderful, Matchless Name of Jesus Christ Our Soon Coming King and The Saviour of Mankind.

Privileged and Blessed am I to be in this Position that allows me to write Inspired Messages for God's People.

Here we have A Topic that is Debatable to many but not for myself, because it has been Revealed to me by God.

Warning! This Topic will cause God's People to take a second look at how we would desire for things to be done.

I've Received this Revelation a long time ago when I was appointed by God to become a Minister for the Gospel of Jesus Christ, but for some strange reason, whenever I bring this Fact to light, I was met with disapproval from those who I seek to share this Revelation with. The time has now come that The Lord Has Now Told me to Write about the Facts of this Revelation. We are going to Start with The Word of God; and for those who also Study their Bible, I would ask that you also search The Scriptures of this

Revelation to identify for yourself that what is being Revealed is actually The Living Truth.

Genesis Chapter 12:1-3.

> **"Now The Lord Had Said unto Abram, Get thee out of thy country, and from thy kindred, and from thy father's house, unto a land that I Will Shew thee: And I Will Make of thee a great nation, and I Will Bless thee, And Make thy name Great; and thou shalt be A Blessing: And I Will Bless them that bless thee, and Curse him that curseth thee: and in thee shall all families of the earth be blessed".**

Every Blessing must have A Foundation from which it springs from, in other words, every Divine Blessing from God, must have A Foundation Seed; A Promise that first came from God to Fulfill with someone, of which this person has done what was Required of them to do, thus Establishing the fulfillment of The Promised Divine Covenant Blessing that The God of The Universe Has Made A Promised to Fulfill.

In this existence of mankind with the governance of that which were governed by, and also looking at the physical manifestation, this person according to Bible studies is none other than our father Abraham. We could have explained that it began with Seth, but The Manifestation of Promised began with Abraham. If we're looking at The Spiritual View, The Foundation then must be God, which filters down in the physical manifestation of Jesus Christ The Lamb of God from which everything Flows Spiritually to establish everything that is seen physically.

Therefore, if there is any Person; People; Nation; Languages; Kingdom and Dominion that requires to Receive of The Divine Blessing that Springs from The Foundation of Abraham's Covenant with God; those who need to receive must Align themselves under the guidelines of that which God Originally Asked Abraham to Fulfill.

Therefore, it must be understood that God Always has a set of People that are Called and Chosen for The Divine Complete Covenant Blessing of that which Abraham is The Foundation of that Blessing. Those set of People by The Revelation of God's Word are Known as The Tithes of The Lord or The Tithes of all People to be Presented to God. The Lord would have for His People to Understand that in all Nations, Kingdoms, Dominions, City, Country, Towns and Languages; there is to be found A Tenth of those people that will Represent The Tithes of People for The Lord; meaning that this Tithes of People will be those who have Aligned themselves in The Covenant Promise of that which Abraham Received. To explain further: The number one Condition for A Child of God who now Desires to become The Tithes of The Lord is that of **SEPARATION,** which is in Fact the word we know as **HOLINESS**.

There is found in the world at present two types of Provisions or Blessing Manifestation from God; they are known as:

1. GOD'S PROVISIONAL BLESSING...

This is making reference to the Cycle of life itself; in the Cycle of life there is found that all people that walk the face of the Earth will experience the Sun rising and that very Sun going down to allow the Moon to rise, then again the moon will set to facilitate the Sun to rise again.

This depends however on the view that a person is looking from. Above the earth there is no rising of the sun or moon but the earth rotates. The Cycle of life demonstrates that the Rain will fall for all people; plants will grow for all people; thus the Fact is that all people will experience the Blessings that comes forth from God's Set Provisional Favors within the Cycle of Life.

Therefore, everyone will receive the benefits of having food to eat and water to drink; all people will have the benefit of having clothes and shoes to wear; many will have the experience of living in a House. And this was what Abraham was originally apart of; life was going on, everyone living their lives according to what they see others doing because everyone is in the same Category of God's Provisional Blessing; which means that no one knows better of that which can be different about their lives, because they are stuck in a Cycle of life that will continue unless God Brings forth The Revelation of Change to that person.

2. GOD'S DIVINE BLESSING...

This is making reference to God's Unique Favors upon the lives of those who have Accepted The Call for their lives to understand that the only way they can in Fact receive of this Special Stamp of God's Divine Favors, is to first find themselves in the Position that they now Understand that there must now be Manifested within their lives the order of Complete Separation from those things that are not Pleasing in The Eyes of God. And this Separation is the Beginning of A Walk of Holiness with God. This person that is walking after Holiness through Separation, will also experience the Provisional Blessing of God's Favor, because all people will experience God's Provision, but not all people will experience God's Divine Favored Blessing. Now this Separation is not going to take place in one step, nor is it going to be experienced within one year of A Christian's Journey or even longer, but as long as we are determined to pursue after separation which leads to holiness, it will be achieved for the Child of God that is determined to obtain their fixed Divine Covenant Blessing in God. Abraham was the Foundation, and he never had as many distractions as we have now, and it took Abraham twenty five years to understand Complete Separation to receive the Continuation of the Promise that God Had Made to him. I don't believe that it will take us the people of God Twenty five years to understand what God's Requirement is for our lives, because we have a lot of examples to know what Separation and Holiness is. And again this is only my Revelation from The Father.

Note: It must be mentioned to Christians; every path of Separation that we Sacrifice to fulfill for God's Holy Walk, this will now Release A New Revelation of God's Divine Relationship with that Child of God. It is revealed in The Book of Genesis Chapter 13:14. The Bible Said:

> **"And The Lord Said unto Abram, after that lot was separated from him, Lift up now thine eyes, and look from the place where thou art northward, and southward, and eastward, and westward: For all the land which thou seest, to thee Will I Give it, and to thy seed for ever. And I Will Make thy seed as the dust of the earth: so that if a man can number the dust of the earth, then shall thy seed also be numbered. Arise, walk through the land in the length of it and in the breadth of it; for I Will Give it unto thee. Then Abram removed his tent, and came and dwelt in the plain of Mamre, which is in Hebron, and built there an altar unto The Lord"**.

I hope it has come to our Understanding that the New Revelation of Blessing can only take place through the only medium of Separation. When we think about it, we are the only Blockage of our Divine Relationship with God, because some things that we hold unto, in our Minds we cannot do without these things or these persons; and it is a Fact, God Will Not Reveal New Relationship and Revelations with **BAGGAGES** that resembles **SIN**.

God's Divine Covenant Blessing Continues…

This is basically speaking about those Fixed Blessings that only a few will have The Testimony to Reveal, those who are in Fact Called and Chosen to represent The Tithes of The Lord, that will no doubt be revealed by their own life's success that God's Blessing is **REAL,** and will also be fixed to express that they've not only received for themselves but have experienced the continual fixed released blessings from The Hands of God that spreads to their children to benefit. There are those in life that worked very hard to receive A Blessing or Success through years of work; only to find that they cannot hold onto that success or blessing that they've worked so hard to receive, because it Requires God's Trained Anointing to Allow for Blessings to Remain. And then there are those who have Positioned themselves in God's Will by means of Separation / Holiness; these Saints of God walk into Opportunities and Favors that are Fixed for Divine Inheritance; which means that, not only will that person that is walking after Holiness Receive The Blessing, but also their children will Receive of The Fixed Blessing and Anointing, only if those children seeks to continue the Walk of Separation and Holiness for God.

Note: A Clue To Simplify The Word Separation:

Stay Away From Those Things That Are Displeasing To Your Father's Relationship With Your Altar's Original Manifestation To God!

IT IS A WARNING!

The very moment God Identify that A Child of God Has started the Walk of Separation which leads to Holiness, that's the very second The Lord Will Put in Effect The Word of His Divine Promise which He Made with Abraham, which Says:

"Those Who Bless You I Will Bless, And He That Curseth You I Will Curse".

Therefore, each Child of God must understand that a walk of Separation which Manifest Holiness is a walk that is filled with The Fixed Benefits of God's Divine Favors; those who don't like you, would have to keep that opinion to themselves, because if they once utter the words of their dislike for you out of their mouth or even conceive it in their Mind and Heart; The God that Keepeth **COVENANT** Will now Manifest upon their own head that which they desire for the Hurt of God's Separated / Holy People.

Now if we remain to be Separated, this now means that we are in God's Eye, A Holy People; which means that because we are Holy, it will bring forth the Manifestation of Divine Blessings upon whatever we put our hands to perform, because of The Spiritual Biding Law of God which is **FIXED** in **COVENANT**. It is therefore identified that a person needs not to desire to be formed in a specific group, or even be born in a specific family, or even attend a special University to be Approved for God's Divine Favors; all that The Lord Would Require from that person is to start the walk of Separation, and this walk must Manifest Holiness, which will bring forth The Fruits of God's Divine Favors.

Now Abraham found himself to be A Blessing because of Obedience that brought Separation, this manifested in God's Favors being continually upon the life of Abraham and all that he had. Even when it came to the point that Abraham Feared for his own life because of his beautiful wife Sarah, God Proved to Abraham that He Does Not Forget About **COVENANT**. Pharaoh was Plagued and Warned by God to return the man's wife or else.

Genesis Chapter 12:17-20.

"And The Lord Plagued Pharaoh and his house with great plagues because of Sarai Abram's Wife. And Pharaoh called Abram and said, What is this that thou hast done unto me? Why didst thou not tell me that she was thy wife? Why saidst thou, She is my sister? So I might have taken her to me to wife: now therefore behold thy wife, take her, and go thy way. And Pharaoh commanded his men concerning him: and they sent him away, and his wife, and all that he had".

King Abimelech fell under the same punishment of Warning from God because of Abraham's Wife.

Genesis Chapter 20:3.

"But God Came to Abimelech in a dream by night, And Said to him, Behold, thou art but a dead man, for the woman which thou hast taken; for she is a man's wife".

Again we see **COVENANT** being Maintained by God because of Abraham pursuing Separation that Leads to Holiness.

Now let us start to understand fully the importance of a person that is Separated for Holiness within the lives of those who they are surrounded by. Within the same Story of Abraham and king Abimelech, it is mentioned in Verse 18.

> **"For The Lord had fast closed up all the wombs of the house of Abimelech, because of Sarah Abraham's wife".**

In Verse 7. It mentioned that God Told Abimelech to let Abraham pray for him, because he is a Prophet. In Verse 17. It Says:

> **"So Abraham Prayed unto God: And God Healed Abimelech, and his wife, and his maidservants; and they bare children".**

Therefore, We've come to the Understanding that Abraham was not a Priest, nor was he in the practice of becoming a Priest according to man's tradition, but because Abraham found himself within The Constitution of God's Law which was Separation that Manifest Holiness, Abraham was immediately Recognized in The Favors of God's Will, to Pray for whomever God Would Desire for him to Pray for, and that Prayer would have brought forth Healing, Deliverance and Blessing to whomever receive of that Prayer from a Person that is Separated for The walk of God's Holiness.

There must also be the understanding to identify that whatever is done to a Child of promise for God's Divine Blessing, that which is done whether good or bad, it would have to follow the Spiritual and Physical practice of seed being sown, therefore, whatever is done to a Child of Separation for God's Purpose will not execute an immediate response from God because all seed that is sown whether Spiritual and Physical, must have the examination of The Father to Identify exactly what seed is sown and what is the purpose of the seed that was planted by whoever have planted that seed. It therefore demonstrates to God's People that this walk of pursuing Separation / Holiness, finding God's Way will never exclude us from the darkness of those who are around us. But **COVENANT** that is made between ourselves and God will always be the Final Judgement.

There must be the understanding in us to know that within every Kingdom govern by a king, there must be found a Religious Entity, meaning a Priest or a person that stands in the Position to Represent God, to Pray for People and the Kingdom, also to be An Anointed Advisor to a king. Now you will notice the importance of Abraham to God as An Intercessor or Mediator, because God Never Told Abimelech to let one of his Priest Pray for him, because God Would Not have Recognized the voice of a person that was not Manifested for the walk of Separation that brings forth Holiness.

There must be birth in us The Revelation of Holiness for our lives unto The God of The Universe. God Is Complete Holiness in His Full Manifestation, therefore, for us to even Attract God to first Listen to our cry and then to Send forth Deliverance, it simply means that we need and must get ourselves in a Position that we are Separated for the Main Purpose of Holiness that God Can Be Entertained to Release His Favors upon that which we Desire for God to Do for us.

Moving on; Now I need to Reveal to my Readers the Importance of how Abraham viewed his Now Special Relationship with God, that only came through the Obedience of Separation which brought forth Holiness, this simple demonstration should spark a light in our understanding to identify that Abraham before God's Separation was not Holy, nor was he at a level with God that would force God to Release Divine Blessings for himself and his continuation. This makes us realize that with God there is always a climb from that which we are currently to that which we can become in God's Separation. In The Book of Genesis Chapter 24:1-9. In Summary it explained that Abraham was now old and knew that he was going to die; The Bible Said that Abraham called one of his eldest most trusted servant to swear by The Lord, The God of Heaven, and The God of Earth, that he would not take a wife for his son of the daughters of the Canaanites, among whom he dwells, but rather to travel to Abraham's home country, from his kindred, and choose a wife from that land.

Now, what I need my Readers to understand is that Abraham was called to separate from his kindred, and dwelled in the land of the Canaanites; a person may have thought that he would have nothing to do with his own kindred, but this wasn't the case. Abraham's kindred was not the worse of people, but God Choose Abraham for Divine Inheritance; therefore, when it came to the point that there must now be a wife for his son, Abraham choose to ask his servant to search for a wife among his own kindred, because even though Abraham's Inheritance was to inherit the land of Canaan, at that point in life there was still the Canaanites in the land, and they were a people that did not know The God that Abraham was Serving, therefore, Abraham could not allow, nor was it his desire to allow his Promised son of Destiny to be joined to a woman of which her people knew not The True And Living God. And if her people Knew not The True Living God, it is common understanding that she also did not know The True Living God.

Therefore, a person of promise and separation to God's Will, will identify Spiritually that being joined in marriage to a person that is not Serving The True Living God would have Spelt the words **SPIRITUAL DECAY** of The Living Relationship that A Child of God has Developed with their God.

You've Been Warned!

I hope this is an Example for those of us who are Training our children; and the Lesson is this: If we Mix our Generation who knows about God with the Generation that knows nothing about our God nor desires to Serve our God, then it is a Fact; the Separation will seize, Holiness will become Un-holiness, which means that The Covenant that God Has Made with us will definitely be **BROKEN.** It should also be observed that when Abraham's servant requested that he would bring Isaac into the land of his kindred, because it would be easier for a woman to choose to marry Isaac if she saw the person who she is to marry. Abraham responded by Commanding his servant that he must never bring his son back into the country of his kindred, because The Promised was only made possible by God unto him through the Obedience of **SEPARATION.** And it did not only apply to Abraham only, but for all The Seed that should come from The lineage of Abraham.

I hope we learned something Valuable! Therefore, it is fully understood that The Blessing from Abraham was now Imparted or Birth into Isaac being the son of Promise from God; this also means that Isaac was now Trained to carry on The Relationship of Separation for God, which resulted in Holiness unto God, which would now Manifest for Isaac and his Inheritance The Continuation of The Same **COVENANT** that God Had Originally Made with his Father Abraham. And let me remind my Readers what The Covenant is:

Genesis Chapter 12:1-3.

"Now The Lord had Said unto Abram, Get thee out of thy country, and from thy kindred, and from thy father's house, unto a land that I Will Shew thee: And I Will Make of thee a great nation, and I Will Bless thee, and make thy name great; and thou shalt be a blessing: And I Will Bless them that bless

25

thee, And Curse him that curseth thee: and in thee shall all families of the earth be blessed".

In other words, any person that chooses to do something of **BENEFIT** to someone who is under Covenant with God; that person will receive for themselves a Continual Favored Blessing that Springs from The Father of Covenant. And at the same time it is Revealed that any person that does something that is not seen to Manifest Blessing for those under Covenant with God; for those persons, they will discover what it means for The Pipe of Favors to be Turned Off from their Lives. That's The Covenant that is upon each and every person that has become **DISCIPLINE** to walk after Separation which will Manifest **HOLINESS UNTO GOD.**

And this was what Isaac Inherited. It was Clearly Manifested in The Scriptures that Isaac, Abraham's son was great, and grew Greater as he became older. It is mentioned in The Book of Genesis Chapter 26:12-16.

"Then Isaac sowed in that land, and received in the same year an hundredfold: and The Lord Blessed him. And the man waxed great, and went forward, and grew until he became very great: For he had possession of flocks, and possession of herds, and great store of servants: and the Philistines envied him. For all the wells which his father's servant had digged in the days of Abraham his father, the Philistines had stopped them, and filled them with earth. And Abimelech said unto Isaac, Go from us; for thou art much mightier than we".

Now let us take a look at **COVENANT** at work for those who will Separate themselves for God; has Isaac followed in the footsteps of his father Abraham. So it was with Abraham, now it became a full Manifestation in the life of Isaac. Verse 23-25 Says:

> **"And he went up from thence to Beersheba. And The Lord appeared unto him the same night, and said, I Am The God of Abraham thy father: Fear not, for I Am with thee, And Will Bless thee, And Multiply thy seed for my servant Abraham's sake. And he builded an Altar there, and called upon The Name of The Lord, and pitched his tent there: and there Isaac servants digged a well".**

GOD'S VISITATION...

The Visitation from our Father is the only thing that will Separate Christians that are Called from those Child of God that are Chosen to become The Tithes for The Lord. Once it is Identified by God that we have become Separated for Holiness; it means that we are set in A Position to now be Entertained by The Appearance of God through The Voice of God. Therefore, God Knows when the enemies rise up against us, and God Is Set for Vengeance because of Covenant; And God Will Make Sure that He Visits His People with Comforting Words, but on the other hand, God Will Visit those who fight against us with Words of Warning that leads to Destruction for all those who have not repented and have a earnest desire to see the hurt of God's Separated, Holy and Covenant Bond People.

It is Revealed in Verse 26-31.

> **"Then Abimelech went to him from Gerar, and Ahuzzath one of his friends, and Phichol the chief captain of his army. And Isaac said unto them,**

Wherefore come ye to me, seeing ye hate me, and have sent me away from you? And they said, We saw certainly that The Lord was with thee: and we said, Let there be now an oath betwixt us, even betwixt us and thee, and let us make a covenant with thee; that thou wilt do us no hurt, as we have not touched thee, and as we have done unto thee nothing but good, and have sent thee away in peace: thou art now The Blessed of The Lord. And he made them a feast, and they did eat and drink. And they rose up betimes in the morning, and sware one to another: and Isaac sent them away, and they departed from him in peace".

"If God be for us, who can be Against us"!

Because of Covenant, Abimelech and his men came and begged for Peace and Covenant between themselves and Isaac. **WOW!** Now it wasn't mentioned in The Bible as it was mentioned for Abraham, exactly what God Said to these men; but we know by experience that God Definitely Came and Visited these men, and I Guess His Words Spoke something in this manner:

1. **"Were you not afraid to cause harm to My Servant"?**
2. **"Did you not consider what I Would Do to anyone that Touched My Anointed"?**
3. **"Go quickly before My Anger Has Peaked; Tell My Servant that you are sorry, and make Peace with My Servant"!**

Now when Isaac was now old, and he knew that he was going to die; just like his father before him, Isaac Knew that he had to set things in order for his son to Continue The Inheritance of The

Covenant Blessing that God Had Originally Imparted upon the life of his Father Abraham.

Through custom it was well known that the Inheritance of the family blessing must be given to the first born; of which Isaac was Fixed to ensure that he would follow Tradition. But The God of The Universe Had Other Plans; Because when the children was in the womb, it was Revealed to Rebckah, Isaac's wife, that there are two Nations in her womb, and the older son shall be servant to the younger son; therefore, even though it was Isaac's desire to bless Esau; According to God's Plan, it wasn't Esau that would Receive The Continuation of The Divine Covenant Blessing, but instead it would have been Jacob. Even before Isaac mistakenly Imparted The Divine Covenant Blessing on Jacob, there were signs that Manifested that God Could Not Have Chosen Esau; the first sign was observed when Esau sold his Birthright to Jacob for Food, Genesis 25:29-34; this Manifestation Revealed that Esau did not Value the Responsibility or Purpose of The Birthright, because he said: Verse 32.

> **"And Esau said, Behold, I am at the point to die: and what profit shall this birthright do to me?"**

The next Manifestation can be seen in The Book of Genesis Chapter 26:34&35.

> **"And Esau was forty years old when he took to wife Judith the daughter of Beeri the Hittite, and Bashemath the daughter of Elon the Hittite: Which were a grief of mind unto Isaac and to Rebekah".**

A Grief of Mind to his Parents, then what about GOD? They may not have told him that they did not approve, because The Bible Said it was a Grief of Mind. It is also Revealed that his Parents being Isaac and Rebekah did not give the Approval, because they had some knowledge about The Covenant Promise. In God's Eye, this second Manifestation of Esau Deeds Revealed what God Already Knew about Esau; therefore, resulting in God's Decision, not to Impart or to Allow Isaac to Impart The Divine Blessing of Covenant on Esau, but rather to be Influence in another Path to Impart The Covenant Blessing on Jacob.

If we could remember how important it was for Abraham to make certain that his Covenant son received a wife from his own country; in that he asked his trusted servant to put his hand under his thigh, and swear by God that he would not allow his son to marry one of the daughters of the surrounding country; because the people of the surrounding country knew not about The Relationship of how to Separate for Holiness in order to Please God. Therefore, Esau choose for himself his own Destiny; because in God's Eye, His Divine Covenant Blessing could never continue upon a Soil which means the woman; such a Soil that knows nothing about God's Divine Covenant Relationship; Even though the man Esau was in Fact of The Lineage of The Divine Seed.

Therefore, this is a Warning for Men that are Serving God with Divine Covenant in View; you cannot Marry those who you choose to marry because they look pretty; rather we should desire to Marry those who Looks like and is of The True Manifestation of God; and this Warning is also being made for the Women under Covenant with God; you just cannot choose who you would desire to Marry for appearance only, that person must have The True Manifestation of God in them. If this is not followed, then we are going to travel on the same road that Esau travelled on, which is the loss of Divine Covenant Blessing.

You Are Warned!

It is also observed that after Jacob Received of The Divine Covenant Blessing. Isaac his father Charged him concerning a wife, this is mentioned in The Book of Genesis Chapter 28:1-4.

> **"And Isaac called Jacob, and Blessed him, and Charged him, and said unto him, Thou shalt not take a wife of the daughters of Canaan. Arise, go to Padanaram, to the house of Bethuel thy mother's father; and take thee a wife from thence of the daughters of Laban thy mother's brother. And God Almighty Bless thee, and make thee fruitful, and multiply thee, that thou mayest be a multitude of people; And give thee The Blessing of Abraham, to thee, and to thy seed with thee; that thou mayest inherit the land wherein thou art a stranger, which God gave unto Abraham".**

Now let us have a look at the Impartation of The Divine Covenant Blessing from Isaac to Jacob, of which it took someone who is already Blessed to Declare or to Impart Blessing on someone else that Desires to Be Blessed.

> **Genesis Chapter 27:26-29.**

> **"And his father Isaac said unto him, Come near now, and kiss me, my son. And he came near, and kissed him: and he smelled the smell of his raiment, and Blessed him, and said, See, the smell of my son is as the smell of a field which The Lord hath Blessed: Therefore God Give thee of the dew of Heaven, and the fatness of the Earth, and plenty of corn and wine: Let people serve thee, and nations bow down to thee: be lord over thy brethren, and**

let thy mother's sons bow down to thee: cursed be every one that curseth thee, and blessed be he that blesseth thee".

Covenant Blessing Transferred, of which it was already God's Plan from The Spiritual but needed a vessel within the physical to bring into fulfillment what is in The Mind of God. The Bible Said in Verse 19&25. That Isaac desired for his Soul May Bless his son, of which he taught it would have been Esau; this means that after Isaac had poured out that type of Blessing, there was no other Blessing of that kind that anyone could have received. And so it was found out by Esau when he came in after to receive the Blessing that his brother had already received. The Bible mentions that Esau cried with a great and exceeding bitter cry, and said unto his father, Bless me, even me also, O my father. Verse 34 of Genesis Chapter 27. Esau begged for a Blessing, but not even begging and crying could have reversed what was already done to Jacob.

Isaac his father basically told him that there is not another Blessing like The Blessing that Jacob Received, because he had already poured out his Soul unto Jacob; that Blessing had in it the Ingredients and also The Seed of Divine Covenant Blessing, of which once it has been Imparted, no one can remove that Divine Blessing, and so it was proven for the entire life of Jacob.

Moving on: In Genesis Chapter 30:22-26. It is reported that Rachel, Jacob's desired wife gave birth to their son Joseph, by this Revelation of The Divine Promised Child, Jacob now realized that he could not grow the child of Inheritance in an environment of Bondage or Slavery, Jacob requested from Laban his father-in-law that he desires now to leave and to go back to the land of his father and forefather Abraham, the land that God Had Promised that He Would Make him to Be A Blessing.

Genesis Chapter 28:13-15.

"And behold, The Lord Stood Above it, and Said, I Am The Lord God of Abraham thy father, and The God of Isaac: the land whereon thou liest, to thee Will I Give it, and to thy seed; and thy seed shall be as the dust of the earth, and thou shalt spread abroad to the west, and to the east, and to the north, and to the south: and in thee and in thy seed shall all the families of the earth be blessed. And, Behold, I Am With thee, and Will Keep thee in all places whither thou goest, and Will Bring thee again into this land; for I Will Not Leave thee, until I Have Done that which I Have Spoken to thee of".

Note: Jacob had other children of the Soil of Leah, but it was not until Jacob received a Seed from The Divine Soil of Rachel, that he decided that it was now time to go on the Journey that His Grandfather Abraham had taken, which is A Journey of Separation which would bring forth an acceptable mark of Holiness before God.

For the life of Joseph, because he was chosen for Divine Inheritance, Joseph had to go through great preparations, and even in those Training, whatever Joseph did, it was a Blessing to whoever he did it for. In Potiphar's house Joseph was the only light to shine to manifest Blessing for that house; in Jail whatever Joseph did, The Lord Allowed it to Prosper, because God Was Fixing Joseph to walk into Divine Covenant Blessing.

There came a time after Joseph was elevated to be A Ruler for Egypt and his family and his people were now where he was. The Bible Mentioned of a time that Jacob was now old, and was soon to die; it was told Joseph, and by Tradition he brought his two sons Manasseh being the eldest son and Ephraim being the younger son,

Joseph brought them to Jacob for the main purpose that his father would continue the Transfer of The Divine Covenant Blessing. Now in the Mind of Joseph, he wanted the eldest son to receive The Divine Covenant Blessing, just like his Grandfather Isaac, but God Had Again A Different Plan, because God Revealed to Jacob that The Divine Blessing must be transferred to the younger son and not the eldest son. This was displeasing in the eyes of Joseph, as he tried to stop what Jacob was doing, because he thought Jacob did not know what he was doing, because his eyes were dim. Jacob however revealed to Joseph that he is aware of what he is doing, and who it is that he is Declaring The Covenant Blessing upon. Jacob told Joseph that Manasseh shall become a great people, and also be great, but his younger brother Ephraim shall be greater than he, and his seed shall become a multitude of Nations. There it is again, Divine Covenant Blessing Transferred on who God Desires for it to Be Transferred upon; and again it took someone who is already Blessed by God to now be in the Position that they can now Bless that person who God Told them to Bless.

Note: This Divine Covenant Blessing was also expressed under the leadership of Moses when Balak the king of Moab requested for a prophet called Balaam to curse God's People, In the book of Numbers Chapter 24:8-9. Covenant recognition was expressed again many years after the foundation Covenant was made from God to our Forefather Abraham.

> **"God Brings him out of Egypt; He has strength like a wild Ox; He shall consume the nations, his enemies; He shall break their bones and pierce them with his arrows. He bows down, he lies down as a lion; And as a lion, who shall rouse him? <u>Blessed is he who blesses you, and cursed is he who curses you</u>".**

Moses was Divinely Fixed and Sanctified by God to Lead out The Children of Israel from Egypt, and did a very good job, but when Moses time was coming to an end, The Lord Told Moses to call for Joshua and Charge him in The Work of The Lord. The Bible Also Said that The Lord Asked Moses to Lay his hands upon Joshua to Imparted The Continuation of The Divine Covenant Blessing; therefore, Joshua would now be able to walk in the Manifestation of The Anointing that Moses found himself to walk in, by the means of Moses Imparting that Blessing of Authority upon the life of Joshua. For all the days of Joshua, Israel succeeded in everything that they put their hands to, as long as they Obeyed the voice of Joshua; and the main reason for that, is because Joshua was now found to Be In Divine Covenant Blessing with God by the Impartation of the hands of Moses through the Request of God Almighty.

Numbers Chapter 27:18-23.

"And The Lord Said unto Moses, Take thee Joshua the son of Nun, a man in whom is the spirit, and lay thine hand upon him; And set him before Eleazar the priest, and before all the congregation; and give him a charge in their sight. And thou shalt put some of thine honour upon him, that all the congregation of the children of Israel may be obedient. And he shall stand before Eleazar the priest, who shall ask counsel for him after the judgment of Urim before The Lord: at his word shall they go out, and at his word they shall come in, both he, and all the children of Israel with him, even all the congregation. And Moses did as The Lord Commanded him: and he took Joshua, and set him before Eleazar the priest, and before all the congregation: And he LAID HIS HANDS

upon him, and gave him a charge, as The Lord
Commanded by the hand of Moses".

Deuteronomy Chapter 34:9.

"And Joshua the son of Nun was full of the spirit
of wisdom; for Moses had LAID HIS HANDS
upon him: and the children of Israel hearkened unto
him, and did as The Lord Commanded Moses".

It is clear to say that whoever Lay their Hands on you, that person
will also Impart something on you that is of their Characteristics. Now
if we are unwise, and are seeking to follow after the Traditions of what
we see most Churches are a custom to do, by allowing any and every
person they desire to Lay Hands on God's People; then we can judge
for ourselves: What do we think we are receiving?_____.

Or I think the Question should be: What do we think that we
are losing when someone who is not Blessed and Anointed by God
comes forth to Lay their hands on you?_____.

We are being Zapped of our Anointing that we took so long
to build in God, through Fasting, Prayer Meetings and Personal
Fellowship with God.

That's the main reason we find many going to Church and
coming back home feeling Worse than how they went in. Some
people that are going to Church, although they may be Christians or
Officials in Church; for many, if they do not have The Relationship
of Covenant over their lives, they **Cannot Bless**; rather they would
have found themselves walking with spirits, Possessed by Demons;
then when it is that they Lay their hands upon us; What do you think
is Transferred!

If it is that through Laying of Hands Characteristics is
also Transferred; What do we think is being Imparted over our
lives?_____.

Again let me Clearly Declare that I'm not against Laying of Hands; I'm rather peculiar about who it is that is doing this exercise. For The Pastor, The Bishop or The Anointed Priest for God, I have no Problem; anyone else, big problem for me. But this is only my Opinion and Revelation from The Father; as I said at the beginning of this Message that this Topic is Debatable, therefore after Reading this Message, I will ask my Readers to think for themselves and choose for themselves. **FREEWILL,** I can't choose for another person.

Now according to Bible Studies, Laying of Hands serves two Purposes.

1. It serves the purpose to Impart on those who desire to receive of that which is being Imparted such as Blessings and Gifts, also the Characteristics of a person as it is seen for the life of Joshua from the hands of Moses, which was Ordered by God.
2. Laying of Hands Serves the Purpose of Removal, as in the prayer to ask God to remove Sins from a person, so was it practiced by the Priest before they went into the Holy of Holies on behalf of the People; and if the Priest was not found to be clean in God's Eye they would have died.

Now the question I would be asking myself if I was reading this Message is: What else can be Removed by this Exercise?_____.

Now, Let us have a look at this, because The Bible Said that My People are Destroyed for A Lack of Knowledge. If you are A Child of God, and you have been Doing The Sanctify before the Sacrifice is Offered to God, and you completely Understand how to Serve God; you've been taught how to do The Accepted Fasting and Prayers; you've been keeping your Personal Relationship with God by Reading The Words of God to Understand what God Needs for you to Understand; you know that your life is at a level with God.

Now this is the Question: How can someone who is not Discipline as you are in your Relationship with God be able to put their hands on you because they believe that speaking in tongues gives them the rights to desire to pray to bless; how and when, if ever, can that person be able to Impart A Blessing upon your life; Now that's my Question?

There is a trend in the Church, that many believe that to be Anointed by God is to make the **MOST NOISE**. The Man of God Bishop Austin Whitfield would often time say:

"Empty Barrels Make The Most Noise".

According to what I've been trying to explain; throughout the history of The Bible where Blessing is concern; there is Nowhere in The Bible it is mentioned that someone who was not Blessed by God was now able to Bless someone else that desires A Blessing from God through Laying of Hands.

NOWHERE IN THE BIBLE!

Now if A Saint of God is not Knowledgeable of the devices of the Devil; we will find ourselves being at a level with God, then Automatically we've been Zapped, Sucked of our Anointing because, if Blessing is not being Imparted when a person place their Hands to pray for you, then what do we think is Happening to us? That's it! Anointing is being Sucked from our Vessel, and we don't even know it. If we are not being Blessed, then is it a Fact, we are being Cursed. I can just hear my Readers saying: Is this Possible, will God Allow this to Happen in His Church? God Gave Adam and Eve The Freewill to Choose; Did He not Do that! God Knew Judas was going to betray Him, it was Fixed; He Said what thou Doest, do Quickly. Wise Christians will always Evolve, Foolish Christians will be Stuck in a Big Circle, going around that Circle for years because they've not learnt that the same steps in life must bring forth the same results all the time.

Samuel the Prophet was Called by God to be an Anointing of Blessing; this was the same Prophet that God Asked to Fill his horn with oil, and go to the house of Jesse The Bethlehemite, because He Had Prepared Himself a king amongst his sons. Samuel went to the Sacrifice, and again we would have discovered that man's will is always Contradicting with God's Will; because Samuel saw Eliab and Immediately wanted to Transfer The Divine Covenant Blessing upon him, But God Stood in the way and Told him not to look on his countenance, because He had Refused him from being king. David was Called, being small and ruddy, not within man's expectation; but when God Chooses, Man is always Astonished. 1 Samuel Chapter 16.

We then discover again, that it took Someone who was Anointed by God to Transfer and make Fixed The Continuation of The Covenant Divine Blessing upon the life of David. Of which, this was the same king David that God Chose to Bring Forth His Divine Seed of Salvation through The Sacrifice of Jesus Christ.

God Used king David when he was old to Stand as a Mediator to declare and to make Manifest The Continuation of God's Divine Covenant Blessing upon the life of Solomon. David commanded to call Zadok the Priest of the day and Nathan the Prophet of the day to Anoint Solomon that he would become the new king of Israel. Divine Blessing Transferred through the Laying of Hands of Someone who is already Anointed for the Purpose to Bless. This event was of great significance, because it was found that one of king David's sons wanted to overthrow him, and self-proclaimed himself to be the new king of Israel.

That son was Adonijah; he was not Knowledgeable to know that the only way he could receive the throne was to go through God's Divine Covenant. He thought he could have just declared himself to be king, and it would have worked; he thought he could have had his own priest, his own followers and supporters; and that would be enough to elevate him to the Level to receive The Divine Mark of Covenant Favored Blessing from God. So he thought, and so it was that he was Rejected by God, just like Esau. 1 Kings Chapter 1. Can be read to explain what took place.

Now that we've exhausted ourselves in The Fundamentals of Foundation which is from the Beginning, meaning Old Testament. Let us have a brief look at the Manifestation of the New Testament. Now it is Declared and Manifested in The Book of St Matthew Chapter 1. Through the Genealogy explanation of Matthew, the Clear Fact that Jesus Christ Came out of the lineage of David and can also be traced right back to the lineage of Abraham and Seth; this therefore brings the discovery of The Continuation of Divine Covenant Blessing upon The Life of Jesus Christ who is in Fact The Full Manifestation of God within **A BODY.**

Because God Is A Spirit, therefore, for God to Fulfill Salvation Plan, He had to be Born in A Spotless Body that knew no sin. It is well recorded in The Gospel The Ministry of Jesus Christ; being The Full Manifestation of God; He Spoke to Situations, Conditions, Demons, Legions and even Death; and they had to Obey His Voice; He did many Miracles by Speaking and by Laying His Hands; because He Represented The Same Voice that Spoke in The Beginning of Time, which Said:

"LET THERE BE LIGHT", and Light came Forth".

The Ministry of Jesus Christ Manifested that through Faith in God, whatever is desired can actually be achieved; however, in many cases, higher level of Deliverance required a higher level of Disciplined Relationship with God. Therefore, The Lord Would Have Us to Understand that all things are truly Possible through Belief in God, but if there is a situation in our life that will not move, it simply means that more Depth in God is Required. The Ministry of Jesus

Christ brought forth Manifestations of Fruits, and that's what we are going to finalize our discussions with.

Acts Chapter 3:1-10.

> **"Now Peter and John went up together into the temple at the hour of prayer, being the ninth hour. And a certain man lame from his mother's womb was carried, whom they laid daily at the gate of the temple which is called beautiful, to ask alms of them that entered into the temple; Who seeing Peter and John about to go into the temple asked an alms. And Peter, Fastening his eyes upon him with John, said, Look on us. And he gave heed unto them, expecting to receive something of them. Then Peter said, Silver and gold have I none; but such as I have give I thee: In The Name of Jesus Christ of Nazareth rise up and walk. And he took him by the right hand, and lifted him up: and immediately his feet and ancle bones received strength. And he leaping up stood, and walked, and entered with them into the Temple, walking, and leaping, and praising God. And all the people saw him walking and Praising God. And they knew that it was he which sat for alms at the Beautiful gate of the temple: and they were filled with wonder and amazement at that which had happened unto him".**

Anointed Fruits from The Ministry of Jesus Christ bringing forth The Characteristics of Jesus Christ even though He was no longer on Earth as a man but as A Holy Ghost Spirit.

Acts Chapter 6:3-7.

"Wherefore, brethren, Look ye out among you seven men of honest report, Full of The Holy Ghost and Wisdom, whom we may appoint over this business. But we will give ourselves continually to prayer, and to the ministry of The Word. And the saying pleased the whole multitude: and they chose Stephen, a man full of faith and of The Holy Ghost, and Philip, and Prochorus, and Nicanor, and Timon, and Parmenas, and Nicolas a proselyte of Antioch: Whom they set before the apostles: and when they had prayed, they LAID THEIR HANDS on them. And the word of God increased; and the number of the disciples multiplied in Jerusalem greatly; and a great company of the priest were obedient to the faith".

Again Blessings of Covenant Promise being Spread and Manifested through the Fruits of The Ministry of Jesus Christ.

Acts Chapter 8:14-24.

"Now when the Apostles which were at Jerusalem heard that Samaria had received The Word of God, they sent unto them Peter and John: Who, when they were come down, prayed for them, that they might receive The Holy Ghost: For as yet he was fallen upon none of them: only they were baptized in the Name of The Lord Jesus. Then LAID THEIR HANDS on them, and they received The Holy Ghost. And when Simon saw that through laying on of THE APOSTLES HANDS

The Holy Ghost was given, he offered them money, Saying, Give me also this power, that on whomsoever I lay hands, he may receive The Holy Ghost. But Peter said unto him, Thy money perish with thee, because thou hast thought that The Gift of God may be purchased with money. Thou hast neither part nor lot in this matter: for thy heart is not right in The Sight of God. Repent therefore of this thy wickedness, and pray God, if perhaps the thought of thine heart may be forgiven thee. For I perceive that thou art in the gall of bitterness, and in the bond of iniquity. Then answered Simon, and said, Pray ye to The Lord for me, that none of these things which ye have spoken come upon me".

Now it is identified that when The Word of The Lord was spread to Samaria, the persons that were called wasn't Ordinary Saints; they called for The Apostles, being Peter and John, Anointed Men of God, who had The Authority, The Foundation and The Blessing of God in them to Manifest The Continuation of Divine Covenant through The Ministry of Jesus Christ. It is also mentioned that these two men Prayed and then Laid their Hands on the people, and the people Received The Gift of The Holy Ghost. Therefore, how is it that many declare that they have received The Gift of The Holy Ghost, when there is no Manifestation from themselves of Holiness to even Attract God much less to receive The Holy Ghost. In a nutshell, The Holy Ghost Must Be Manifested, and this Manifestation Cannot Lie or Hide.

Acts Chapter 9:15-18.

"But The Lord Said unto him, Go thy way: for he is a chosen vessel unto me, to bear My Name before the Gentiles, and kings, and the children of Israel: For I Will Shew him how great things he must suffer for My Name's Sake. And Ananias went his way, and entered into the house; and PUTTING HIS HANDS on him said, Brother Saul, The Lord, even Jesus, that appeared unto thee in the way as thou camest, hath sent me, that thou mightiest receive thy sight, and be filled with The Holy Ghost. And immediately there fell from his eyes as it had been scales: and he received sight forthwith, and arose, and was baptized".

Acts Chapter 19:1-7.

"And it came to pass, that, while Apollos was at Corinth, Paul having passed through the upper coast came to Ephesus: and finding certain disciples, He said unto them, Have ye received The Holy Ghost since ye believed? And they said unto him, We have not so much as heard whether there be any Holy Ghost. And he said unto them, Unto what then were ye Baptized? And they said, Unto John's Baptism. Then said Paul, John verily baptized with the baptism of repentance, saying unto the people, that they should believe on Him which should come after him, that is, on Christ Jesus. When they heard this, they were Baptized in The Name of The Lord Jesus. And when Paul had LAID HIS HANDS upon them, The Holy Ghost Came on them; and they spake with tongues, and prophesied. And all the men were about twelve".

This Revelation is the view of The Ministry of The Church of Jesus Christ Fellowship, Savannah Cross, Jamaica, West Indies. A

Revelation from The God of The Universe Jesus Christ The Lamb of God. Now what does your Revelation Reveals about the same Topic, as I said at the Beginning, it is debatable for many but not for me because I've Identified exactly what God has Revealed to me through the Divine Manifestation of **THE GODHEAD**. To The God that continues to open the eyes of his people to understand the mysteries of Eternal life, to Him be All Glory, Honor and Praise, from Spiritual to Physical then back to The Spiritual, Amen. From Pastor Lerone Dinnall. May God's Divine Covenant Blessing be in your life and the life of your Generation, Amen.

If God Has Anointed You To Become A Divine Covenant Blessing, Then You Can Bless Others; If God Has Not Anointed You For Divine Covenant Blessing, You Cannot Bless Anyone, FACTS!

How Do I Reach Out To Get Intimate With God?

Message # 11   **Written in the year 2015.**

Greetings in The Wonderful Name of Jesus Christ Our Soon Coming King; I count this another opportunity as a privilege to write unto God's Wonderful People.

We have here a Topic that God Has Allowed me to Discern and to come to the conclusion that this is a Topic that not many people or should I say Saints, do not understand what the process is for an individual to reach out and to get connected with God. I sat in Church one day, and The Lord Asked me to look, so that I could realize that there are members in my assembly that just do not know what it is like for a person to Reach out and Touch even The Garment of The Almighty God.

Now this raised some concerns for me; because if I'm to be the Pastor of an Assembly I need to make sure that I do a good job thus making certain that The People of God are well educated of the Reasons and of the Functions of why they must, when they come to the place of Worship put themselves in a position that they ascend to that place that they will Receive A Touch from The Almighty God.

I would like to begin this Message in this fashion: When we come to Church for the purpose of approaching God; is it not for a Reason and for a Purpose?_____. We don't just come to Church for coming sake; many of us come to Church because we believe and have heard that it is the place that a person can be Delivered; can be Healed; can be Washed from all our sins and most importantly we can be Saved. But many of us don't realize that a lot of the reasons that we attempt to come to Church for; Requires that there is A Releasing of God's Anointing upon our lives for all these Miracles to be Performed. And we have not yet considered that there must be an action that comes from us the individuals, that causes this Releasing of this Anointing to be Realized upon our lives.

Do you think that God Openly Releases His Anointing of Blessing and Healing and Deliverance and Saving Grace for no reason at all? There are many Saints that are not knowledgeable of the fact that God Is very much Interesting in a Believer having A Personal Relationship with Him. Just as how Wives have relationships with their Husbands and Husbands their Wives; God Is Searching for Believers that are Disciplined and Ready to be in A Relationship with God. Can you just imagine, everything that you could ever need God to Do for you is already in His Hands, waiting for you to Touch Him and to say here I am Lord, I am present in Your House of Worship. Many people believe that just being in God's Presence is the only thing that is important;

I was at Church today, and that was good enough!

Being present is good, but being in Relationship with God when you're in His Presence goes a lot deeper than the surface.

"Someone Touched Me; Someone Touched Me! Jesus Said"!

Are you the person that God Is going to Recognize the next time you enter the place where His Presence Dwells? Will God Say:

"You have Touched Me".

What we've got to understand is that, whenever there is A Touch; immediately there is A Releasing of The Anointing of God flowing from The Virtue that is in Him, and this is an Anointing that no one can stop, because this Anointing now becomes your Relationship with God. This is the reason why we find that many Saints come to Church and remain the same;

because they came and presented themselves but they forgot about **The Touch**. This Touch is not to touch the Bench or the Altar or even the Microphone physically to give a testimony, or even to come to make sure that the Pastor sees that your present at Church; this Touch that I'm talking about is that which comes Spiritually and with a True Intention to Touch God that will enable The Blessings to Flow, which brings forth The Deliverance that Satisfies every situation.

We are reminded by The Scriptures that God Is A Spirit and they that Worship Him must Worship in Spirit and in Truth; St John Chapter 4:24. This passage of Scripture Brings forth the true essence of how a Saint of God should come before God to offer The Sacrifice of Worship that will be Accepted; anything other than Spirit and Truth will not be Accepted. I remember when my Bishop usually preached this Message; He would Say:

**God Is Searching your hearts when you come
to Him, for Spirit and Truth; and not the opposite
which is Flesh and Lie.**

I never forgot those teachings, and it reminded me of what was the true purpose of coming to Church. There are some who believe that Church can be treated like anywhere else that you happen to attend; this belief is in fact a great error. Church must be treated has the most important place that you could ever attend, has it represent the place where The Holy God Dwells; and if Church is not treated as a place where The Holy God Dwells, then it simple means that the place where you go to Worship is not a Church, but instead it is a building where people gather to have their communion and their own fellowship. You will find yourself in an environment like this mainly pleasing yourselves instead of God.

There are many people who have been to The CourtHouse and has the experience of hearing when they announce the entrance of the Judge; you would have seen and realized that once the Judge is about to enter the Courtroom, there is an announcement that says let us all rise; and all that are present in that Court has to rise or else they would be found to be in Contempt of Court Rules.

I only had one experience of being in a Court of Law, and what I realize from that which I have stated is that when a person goes before the Judge to bring forth their case, you have got to make sure that you dress appropriately or else you will be charged with a fine that must be paid or else you will spend the night in jail; this is what I have seen for myself.

When I consider the great discipline and honour that is shown for another human being as myself; (All respect to the Judge, He or She deserves their honour). But when I consider it and compare the honour that is given to a Judge who is but just a man as myself; and the honour that is given to God The Almighty, when a person comes into His Presence The House of Worship; then I realize that many of us that say we are serving God, Really and Truly don't understand The Importance of God's Presence, and have not yet started to begin Worship, much less to Serve.

Worship is a state of being ready to perform that duty in Spirit and in Truth, which results in A Touch; you the individual Touching God and God in return Touching you, that brings forth a Release of A Special Anointing; being a Servant is a continual effort of being A Worshipper.

What this is saying is that many saint have experienced what it feels like to Worship for one occasion, but when they try to relive the experience, they now realize that Worship has grown; therefore, if your Spiritual life does not grow, it simple means that you're not a servant that will continue to experience Worship in Spirit and in Truth.

Fact: Not everyone that says they are A Christian is indeed A Christian; not everyone that says they are A Servant is indeed A Servant; did not The Bible Say that not all Israel are Israelite. and again, there are a lot of people who has good discipline by the training of their parents that have not committed themselves for the Christian's walk, that are indeed living good acceptable lives, even better than that which some of us as dedicated Christians find ourselves currently living.

This I have seen and experienced for myself. What I am saying is that we need to stop being only focused on what people are saying and rather seek to know them by their works. If you seek to examine a hundred people to ask them if they are living a good life for God, I guarantee that you will have up to 90% giving you a positive response. But in reality and according to God's Standard you may be lucky to even find five persons out of the hundred that truly measure up.

According to Genesis Chapter 18:20-33. There were many people living in the Cities of Sodom and Gomorrah, that was under the influence of sin; and even though our Father Abraham beseech God to search for at least ten persons who was righteous; and if God Was Able to Find at least 10 righteous, He Promised Abraham that He Would Not Destroy the cities. We all know this Story, God Was Not Able to Find the ten, He Couldn't Even Find five that was righteous; Four it was that came out of the city, Lot's wife look back and became a pillar of salt; therefore, it was only three that survived the experience of that dreadful event.

I gave this demonstration to let you know that the next time you come to Church to Worship God, make sure that your focus is on

God, because if you stop to look on anything else, then you may find yourself being a part of 100% of people saying that they are in The House of God to Worship; or it may be that you find yourself being a part of the 50% whose job is to be a pillar of salt in God's House to make sure that they watch other members.

Think about this, in A Church Assembly that is filled to its capacity, do you know that it is about 10% of the whole Church that is truly Worshipping God; 50% are what you can call Watchers; 30% to 40% are attending The Church because of benefits; was it not Jesus Christ which Says:

"Ye follow me not because of the Miracle, but because Ye were fed".

Another 5% to 10% are attending Church because they like The Church or they may like the Pastor and how he Teach and Preach. All this is valuable information that we should know how it is that we are going to identify which part of the percentage we are? I don't know about you, but I know that the 10% that is Worshipping God, I am a part of it; so should each and every Child of God be desirous to be a part of The True Worship Group. Learn this about Saints that are Truly Serving God:

NOTHING CAN STOP US, WE ARE DETERMINE!

Make sure the next time you go before God to Worship, if there is one person that is in the whole congregation according to God's Standard that is Worshipping, that one person is definitely you; make sure that you don't leave unless you have Received your Touch from God. There is no way we'll receive the understanding that Worshipping God involves watching other people; rather than watching others, make sure the only watching were doing is to watch

God and ourselves or watch others for the good examples only to develop A True Relationship with God; because The Bible Says:

> **"Let every man work out his own Salvation**
> **with fear and trembling".**

One of the main reason why I don't Teach Saints to watch other Saints is because every person's Experience and Touch from God comes in a different way; therefore, you may be looking on someone to see how they Worship, and your way to Worship God may just be passing you by; and it is at that same time God Needs to Touch you in a different way. Therefore, I Encourage Saints to find your Personal Relationship with God, of which you will receive your Personal Touch from God.

Learn this, that Touch from God is an Experience that no one can take away. God Is A Spirit, it simple means that God Cannot be seen or felt with our Natural Eyes and Hands; therefore, if this is the case, we have got to realize that, in order for a person to actually Worship God, we have got to train our Minds, Hearts and Bodies, to reach that place that we have cancelled out all evidence of flesh and natural being for that Experience of Worship which is Supernatural or above all that you have ever Experience.

Shirley the song writer says:

> **"When We have received A Touch from God,**
> **you can never be the same".**

What I find interesting is that I have people that have told me that they are afraid to reach out and to Touch God; because they are afraid of what will happen; and even if they are in the process of receiving A Touch, they quench The Presence of God's Hand upon their life, and have confessed that, such an experience is the reason why they have not come back to Church because they are not fully ready to give their lives over unto God. While I respect the honesty of people; it made me realize that Worshipping God is a duty reserved for people who have been Transformed by The Gift of The Holy Ghost to become Saints of God that are Serious.

If you're not A Saint of God; if you're not Determined; if you're not Willing to be Trained; then it is certain that you will never have the appetite to Worship God in Spirit and in Truth, or even to keep Saved. There is one thing that I have proven to be factual, this is it, that Worship begins within a man's own vessel, then it branches off in our Homes; there is a saying that goes like this:

"You have to learn to dance a yard, before you dance abroad".

There is also a saying which Says:

"The Home Is The First Institution For Learning".

Many of us come to Church to start The Fire, but truth be told, The Fire, which is The Operation of The Holy Ghost should have been burning in us before we left the home. Therefore, when we come to Church we would then add fuel to The Fire that is already at Church from the fire that is currently burning within us. This is a fact, many people only Pray when they get to Church; they only Sing when in Church; they only Fast because they are coming to Church; many people, the only time they open The Bible to read a Scripture is when the Pastor tell them to turn their Bible to a particular verse; what I'm saying is that many of us that confess that we are Christians, know nothing about having A Personal Relationship with God.

Therefore, without knowing God for ourselves, it makes Worship that more difficult to achieve when we come into The Presence of God. The song writer says:

"In His Presence there is fullness of joy, and at His Right Hand there are pleasures forever more".

And this is how we Sing this song to describe The House of God. But let me ask a question: Who is it that allows that Presence of God to be in The House of The Lord?_____.

The man in The Mirror can Answer that question; we are The Vessels that are Filled with His Glory, that Enables The Glory of God to Remain in His House. And if we are not aware of what must be done to Entertain The Spirit of God, we may find ourselves losing the Experience of what it truly means to feel The Presence of God in The House of The Lord.

There is one fact that cannot be overlooked where Worshipping is concerned, and this is it; Psalms 51:17. The Sacrifices of God Are A Broken spirit: A Broken and a Contrite Heart, O God, thou Wilt Not Despise. Just look at this for a minute, Jesus Said: Someone Touched Me, because He Said The Virtue has left His Body; the meaning for the word Virtue according to The Bible Dictionary means Power and Strength. How many times when we are Worshipping God, it is realized that the essence of our Virtue has left our body? Many times the Virtue that leaves our body comes in the form of a Teardrop. The Songwriter caught the vision when he explained to us that tears is a language that only God understands.

Look at this Revelation that The Lord Gave to me:

"The Absence of A TEARDROP brings forth the ability of SELF".

God Did Not Design us to be Self-sufficient, but rather Reliant on His Mercy and His Power to be Performed upon our lives. There are many Christians that cry inwardly and in their secret chamber, but what is important for us to remember is that God Recognizes the language that we are uttering unto Him whether in secret or openly. What many of us as Christians fail to realize is that God Is Not A Fool, He Knows who it is that actually comes to Worship Him, because one of the main function of The Spirit of God is to Feel, so that He Can Put whatever is offered to Him on His Measuring Scale to See if that which is offered truly has the correct weight that is suggested by the person that is offering the sacrifice to Him.

There are many of us, because we can put ourselves together and make ourselves look presentable. We are caught in a world where we fool a lot of people; but wake up! There is no man living or has lived, or will ever come to live that will have the capacity to fool The Almighty God. God Knows exactly who everyone is. The sad thing about it is that not many of us actually know Who we are. Fact, the true nature of a man is not what you see on the outside, but that which you are on the inside; it is not what you do to let others see you; it is more what you do in secret and not looking for a reward.

This is the reason why Worship is so very important, because it is within Worship that a person does express to God who they truly are. Learn this, the outer man can never Worship God, but rather offer Praise that leads towards Worship unto God; it now takes the Inner man to bring forth A True Characteristic before God that God Will Accept your Worship once it is done in Spirit and in Truth. Many times you wonder at the Blessing that someone is experiencing from God, but don't stay there and wonder, take a look at their Sacrifice of Worship, then you will fully understand why that person's life is so Blessed.

This Topic is speaking unto each and everyone of God's Children, to let us know that Worship Is A Must, and if there is any person that has lost their Sacrifice to Worship, it's time to get it back;

because without Worship, who are you?_____. And I can answer that question, you're just a shell, let me speak also to myself; we are just a shell, if we do not know how to Worship God.

Worship is a Training, you have to Practice and Learn to do it better each day, so that you will become perfect in becoming A True Worshipper for The Almighty God, not for a season but for Eternity. There is not one direct answer to explain Worship, because it is found that with different vessels the experience of Worship to God manifests itself differently, but the most important thing to achieve is the sure experience of True Worship, whatever form it takes. A Child of God needs also to remember that once they have learnt worship, be very careful, because you can also lose worship, and if we lose our worship, it means that we have lost our sure connection to The Spiritual of Unlimited Benefits from God. Once A Child of God Finds worship or is **BORN** into worship, they are going to **KNOW**, because the experience of just a small portion of worship is so strong that it can never be denied.

In closing, here are a few words to allow us to understand what is required to obtain the experience of **TRUE WORSHIP**.

Become the 10%, which is The Holy Tithes of The Lord wherever we are Identified:

- **By ourselves,**
- **At Home,**
- **At Church,**
- **At Work,**
- **With our Friends,**
- **In the Dark,**
- **In the Light,**
- **In Prayer,**
- **In Fasting,**
- **For Service**
- **In Life**

- **And for the final rest; In Death, so that we can renew our Upright Position in The Spiritual.**

I Thank you all for being a part of this Wonderful Message, and I hope you have been Inspired to continue being A True Worshipper for The Almighty God. God's Blessing upon you and your Family always, Amen. In The Wonderful Name of Jesus Christ, Our Soon Coming King; I remain your Friend, Pastor Lerone Dinnall.

How Do I Reach Out To Get Intimate With God?

Getting To The Level That You're Willing To Move To God's Every Command...

Message # 10
Date Started September 8, 2016
Date Finalized September 10, 2016.

Greetings in The All Powerful Name of Jesus Christ, happy am I to be writing for you another Wonderful Message Inspired by The Mighty Hands of our Lord Jesus Christ. I was in my bed on the same morning of September 8, 2016, when this Topic came to me like a flood, I got up immediately and began to write the Instructions that The Lord Have for me to write at about 2:15 AM in the morning. We all must know by now, that whenever God Gives A Topic, it is for us to do our best to understand what The Lord Is Saying through that Topic, because it is a Fact that God Is Bringing forth A Revelation in our lives that will only be accomplish through the Obedience of those His Servants who are Willing to Obey His Every Command.

In some ways, this Topic reminds me of a Message The Lord Gave couple months Back; the Message was Receiving the Spirit of Obedience. As we have discovered through that previous Message; that to Obey God is not only a skill, but it is indeed a Spirit that a Person actually receive from God, that brings forth a Mindset and Discipline, that whatever God Ask you to do; you're going to make the Freedom of Choice to Do Exactly what He Asked you to Do.

I tell you the truth, those of us who are Servants of The Living God, are in for a well-controlled drive with God The Father being The Captain of our ship. Living a life for God and also reading about what the Servants of The Lord was prepared to do being God's Instrument; this made me realize that Serving God is the highest Job or Sacrifice that anyone could ever seek to do. I know that this World teaches us about the different levels and qualities, also qualifications of various job titles, but the job of a Servant of The Lord Far Exceed all other jobs, although the Qualification to do God's Will is fixed only in one word, and that one word is **OBEDIENCE.**

Therefore the job that a Teacher, a Doctor, a Lawyer, a Governor and President or even a Judge, cannot even come into comparison to the job that A True Servant of God has to Perform. While there is space or tolerance given to these professions to make a mistake, and it then can be corrected or looked over; there is absolutely no Tolerance given to those who esteem themselves to be Servants of The Living God. Let me remind you of the Story in The Bible that Moses the Great leader that he was, is told to speak to the Rock; and instead of speaking to the Rock, he smote the Rock twice. Even though Moses would have had an excuse as to why he was angry because of how the people behaved, this is very important for us to understand; that which God commands for a servant to Do, in any situation or challenges, make sure you do exactly what God Ask you to Do; or else!

Numbers Chapter 20. In this same Chapter you will realize that Aaron the Priest of God died; The Scripture Made sure to give the reason why The Lord Put him to Death; in verse 24, The Lord Said:

"Ye Rebelled Against My Word at the water of Meribah".

There is A Story in The Book of 1 Kings Chapter 13, otherwise known as the story of the disobedient prophet; I remembered before I was Called to do A Work for The Lord, that The Lord Reminded me of this example, to let me know that He's Sending me to do a work for Him, but I must remember that the work is only to Please Him and not myself, therefore, Whatever He Ask me to Do, that must I Do; I remember clearly The Lord Said unto me that not everyone is going to get Saved; therefore, Don't be disappointed if you don't see people changing their lives, because you shall be a witness unto them, that they did hear The Gospel and choose not to Serve God.

The Lord Also Made me know that a lot of people are going to hell, but I must Preach, that it can be said that The Community of Savannah Cross in May Pen Clarendon Jamaica West Indies, had someone that was Preaching to them The Gospel of Jesus Christ as Lord and Saviour. Therefore, Although I would like to see a lot of people coming to Church to Serve God; I found out that, that is not my Mission; my Mission is to Preach The Word of God, that a Foundation of Righteousness can be Established in Savannah Cross, that people will see The Light of the World in us, that they can have no excuse but to come and be born in The Church, to become a part of The Light that Shines in His People.

The Lord Told the Prophet to do a job for him; he was not to eat any food or to drink any water; he was not even to journey the same way he entered from. This prophet allowed an older prophet to persuade him, to let him believe that The Lord Gave him Instructions also to tell him the younger Prophet that he should eat and drink; to do exactly what The Lord Told him Not to Do. I listen to Bishop Austin Whitfield Preached on this Message on a particular day, and this is what he summarized in the story:

"If God Was Able to Give me clear Instructions of not to eat or to drink, and to travel a different way coming back; then the same God that gave me

**all those Instructions, if He was going to change
His Mind to Give me other Instructions, then He
would have to come to me directly as He did at First;
no one is going to change my Mind from what God
Told me to Do".**

I believe Bishop Austin Whitfield; may God continue to Bless
his Work, he was completely correct. I am happy for this story
about the disobedient Prophet, because it makes me a lot wiser in
everything that I would desire to perform for The Lord. We know by
now that we are in the Dispensation of Grace; therefore, The Lord Is
Not as Strict to Condemn anyone to death, but Seeks rather to Offer
chances after chances, to see if there is an expectation of change in the
lives of not only Sinners, but also in the lives of Saints.

But there is one FACT that The Lord Has Revealed to me, and
it is that; every time A Child of God Refuses to Obey or come up
to a level that will allow them to receive of The Spirit of Obedience;
then that Child of God enters **A CYCLE** that allows them to start
the event all over again. It's like living a day all over again, until you've
learned to correct the mistakes of that which you should have done on
that given day. Many of us as Children of God are not knowledgeable
of this Fact; we get older but still remain fixed in the position of
no Spiritual growth for God; never realizing that the reason why
we keep doing the same thing over and over is because we are not
growing into obedience that will cause us to be **WISE**. The Children
of Israel 40 years journey began the first day they disobeyed God;
walking in the Wilderness, growing Physically but dying Spiritually;
eating food; raising their children that will one day be the benefits of
what they should have received, not knowing that all along they were
just walking in a big circle; **A CYCLE** that lasted for 40 long years, all
because they choose not to Obey The Voice of The Lord.

Samuel spoke to king Saul and Said:

"To Obey is better than Sacrifice". 1 Samuel Chapter 15:23.

I find it quite ironic that many Saints actually want to find out what God Will Do to them if they disobey; this is Stupid and Insane, why would I want to Tempt or to Anger The God of all Universe; The God that Says: My Name Is Jealous; I Am A Consuming Fire. Have you ever felt the heat that comes from a fire?____. That's just the heat, what if we got burnt? Then compare that burn to the level of which you're going to be burnt by God. I am seeking to do my best to elevate my thinking to a level, that as long as I know for sure that The Lord Commanded me to Do something; I don't care what it is, because everything that God Ask you to Do, must Represent Him, especially in this Dispensation that God's Requirement is for us to Be Holy as He Is Holy.

A Camel like Attitude; being dumb for God. I guess this is the only place you can use the word dumb, and it is ok. I did some research on the Camel; it is said that a Camel is 100% obedient to the call and direction of his master; for example if you're riding a Camel and there is a fire in the path; if you bid the Camel to go through the fire, the Camel will obey your command; not considering that he is going to cause harm to himself; other animals are not of this character, nor human beings.

The Bible Said:

"That it is easier for a Camel to go through a needle's eye, than for a rich man to enter into The Kingdom of God".

This The Lord Said to make Manifest that a Camel will always seek to do the things that is commanded of him to do, no matter how difficult it may be; although it seems to be impossible to everyone else. Therefore, I find myself asking God for a Camel like Attitude, when it concerns His Will. This Message is speaking to all God's People.

How many times do we give God an excuse as to why we cannot fulfill His Requirements? Let me share with you a parable, which is a True story. I remembered when my wife was about to give birth to our first child Charity in Canada, and I was refused entry in that country. At the time for her to give birth, the baby refused to come forth, that the doctors at the hospital was speaking about C-Section; I remembered Praying and asking God to Deliver my baby safely without C-Section; I felt like my Prayer wasn't enough, therefore, I called my Mother, and Bishop Burke to help me Pray. They Prayed with me but I was still desirous of more Prayer; I then called my Grandmother in New Jersey, told her the situation, she Prayed also; but there was something she said that stuck with me; She said Minister don't worry, when the time Has come for the Baby to come forth, the Baby will come, and **nothing can stop it**.

The baby came forth that same night, without the need of a C-Section, because the time for the baby to come was just the time Appointed by God; she was born on the birthday of the Man of God, Bishop Austin Whitfield, to allow me to have a lifetime reminder of my Grandfather. I shared this story with you to let you know that if you truly have a Spirit of Obedience, then whenever God Gives to you His Commandment; then that Word must break through your personal will, and desire to bring forth that which God Has Commanded you to Do, **and nothing can stop it**; because you're already A Product of God's Will.

- The Lord Said: "Let there be light"!
  Did it happen?_____.
- The Lord Said: "Lazarus come Forth"!
  Was he raised from the Dead?_____.

- The Lord Said to Peter: "Upon this Rock I Will Build My Church, and the Gates of hell shall not prevail against it"! Was The Church Built; is The Church in existence today? _____.

- The Lord Said: "I Will Not Leave you nor Forsake you, even to the end of the world I Will Be With you"! Has He ever left Us?_____.

He Spoke, and it was done, He Commanded, and it stood still. Fact: The reason why we often fail to Obey God's Commandment is because there is no evidence of The Word of God in us, therefore, The Word Cannot connect with The Word.

If we find ourselves still struggling to do some of that which God Commands us to Do; it is because we have not reached the level of understanding, that will Basically birth within us **THE WILLPOWER** that will **DRIVE** us to perform that which God Ask us to Do. Everything in life has a Foundation, and if there is something wrong with your Development; then you've got to stop for a minute and take a closer look at your Foundation that your building on; and if you recognize that your Foundation is not being built on The Word of God; then it's time for you to jump off that Foundation, and begin immediately to build on The True Foundation that cannot be Shaken. The Lord Said:

"Heaven and Earth shall pass away, but My WORD Shall Never Pass Away".

This is **THE TRUE FOUNDATION,** The Word of God. Do you Love His Word or do you despise The Word of God? _____. This answer will give you a clear idea of the reason why we find it so difficult to do what God asks us to Do. If we Love The Word, we Love God, because God Is The Word; God Is Love, therefore, those of us who Love The Word of God, will always have the appetite of needing to Fulfill all that God Asked us to Do. If we don't Love The Word, then there is absolutely no desire in us to perform that which God Asked us to perform. Therefore, We fall right back into Training; **The CYCLE,** living that day all over again, until we've learnt to do what God Asked of us to Do.

Especially if we are a person that is Chosen by God to Perform A Duty for Him.

Being a True Servant of God, there is one main thing that we must learn; and that lesson is how to be **OBEDIENT**. Another way to spell the word Obedient Is:

JUST DO WHAT IS COMMANDED BY GOD.

Trust me, it will cause you a lot less Disappointment, Headaches, Struggles, and not to mention Time. Let us not become like Jonah, who thought that he could actually run from The Presence of God; and found himself in the Belly of a Fish for three days and three nights. If he was not born in the understanding that he needed to Repent of the wrong which he had done, then he would not have been released from the belly of the Fish. Jonah, realizing that God's Charge was not to be taken lightly; entered Nineveh by one day, when the journey to reach Nineveh from where he was should have taken him three days, happily delivered The Message that God Had for him to Deliver.

Jonah being The Tool that he was in The Eyes of God; was the only person God Chose to Use; because by the **WARNING** of his mouth, the people of Nineveh, believing the Message, turned from their wicked ways; Repented of their sin. The king heard of the Prophecy of 40 days then destruction; he got off his royal throne, took off his royal robe; made a decree, that the whole kingdom should seek The Face of God in Fasting and Prayer, and if it was reported that someone did not Fast; then that person whether small of big; human being or animal; that person or animal should be put to death.

Servants of God that are Obeying God, these are the Servants that Saves a lot of lives.

The Bible said that more than One hundred and twenty thousand (120,000) people were saved in Nineveh; this was by the **FORCED OBEDIENCE** of Jonah. Although the story had a nice ending; the experience that Jonah went through to learn was not desired. Servants of God, Sons of God; do we need God to **FORCE** us to **OBEY** Him? There is a lot of people to be Saved, a lot of people that still need to hear of this Gospel's Message; a lot of people that still need to see The Light of Christ in us; are we going to let these people die in their sin; or we going to fail God by disobeying what He Command us to Do.

Let us not look back and say what if I had Preached to that man, or to that woman; what if I had spoken to my Church brother or to my Church sister; what if I had given a word of Encouragement; What if; What if. Let's stop saying What if; and let us start to Do. Ezekiel Chapter 3:15-21 warns us that are Serving God, by letting us know that we are **WATCHMAN.**

Be that Watchman for your brother and sister; be a Watchman for your Minister and Missionaries; and dare I say be also a Watchman for your Pastor. How many times you know of Traps and Snares that are set to destroy a soul, and you say nothing about it. But instead you say to yourself, let me watch and see if he is going to see it for himself; when you are the person that The Lord Revealed it to, for you to save the life of A Potential Child of The Kingdom.

The song writer said, somebody Prayed for me, they had me on their Mind, they Sacrificed their time, they went down on their knees and Prayed for me. Are we standing by and counting all those who are going to hell?_____. What if when we were to get Saved, the person who Prayed for us just stood by and said, anything that should happen let it happen to you.

Let us be a Generation that Cares; even as God Cares for us that He Gave His Only Begotten Son, that whosoever believeth in Him should not perish but have Everlasting Life. I believe that whoever receives this Message, God Has Appointed you to be **A WATCHMAN** for Him, to go out and try your very best, to see how many Souls you can Influence to come to The Lord.

Heaven is not going to be filled by only those who are going to Church; because some of those who are in The Church are still not Worthy for The Marriage Supper, and if this is so, then we have a lot of work to do. Therefore, Go out to the Highways, in the Streets, Lane and Corners; be an Influence; don't matter if the individual doesn't want to come to your Church, as long as they find themselves going to a Church. Have we not read in The Bible:

> **"Other sheep I have which is not of this fold;**
> **them also I must bring that there will be one fold**
> **and one shepherd".**

Do your job and Let God Do the rest. Every Church, as long as they are calling upon God, has a Revelation of Who God Is; some churches just have more Revelation of God than others; but if you enter A House of God, I Guarantee that The Sermon will not be giving Praise to the devil. Let us throw the dirty style out the window, when we say, if he or she is not coming to my Church, then I have no time speaking to them about God. The Lord Gave us a Command, He Said:

> **"Let your Light so Shine before men, that they**
> **may see your good works and Glorify your Father in**
> **Heaven".**

Our job is not to choose for individuals, but only to be The Light of the World. The World can only identify God based on what they see us do. If there is no Light Shining in us, then they cannot see any Manifestation of God through us. But if they just see a little Light to Shine, then they will wake up each morning believing that

God Exist, and He Is Living in us; one more reason for them to give their life over to God.

Let us do all in our power to Obey God, and one of the main things that God Is Seeking from us to do, is to seek for Souls to be added to The Kingdom of God; with each Soul that makes it into God's Kingdom, that's another Star in your Crown. Persuading Souls to give over their lives to God is in no way easy; but you can be certain that God Is Going to Make every effort that we have spent on one Soul, more than worth the effort by Releasing Great Rewards.

Can you just imagine, even for myself, how many lives this very Message would have touched, that it brings forth a Complete Change. Can you imagine, being a Pastor of an Assembly, Teaching and Preaching, and even if it's just ten (10) persons; that's ten people that received of my Effort; my Sweat; my Studying of The Scriptures; with God Giving the Increase, that allowed those ten (10) people to believe in God, that one day they can enter The Kingdom of Heaven. Just writing and speaking about it brings a smile to my face.

This Message is for all of us; let the desire to Obey God, to Work for Him to bring Souls into His Kingdom also put a smile on your Face; let's do it together, play your path in God's Kingdom.

All Honour to The All Powerful Name of Jesus Christ. From the Servant of God and the Ministry of The Church of Jesus Christ Fellowship, Savannah Cross, Jamaica, West Indies. I remain your Brother, Your Friend, Your Fellow worker in the Vineyard and Watchman, Your Pastor, Lerone Dinnall, God's Blessing Continually, Amen.

Getting To The Level That You're Willing To Move To God's Every Command...

What Does It Mean For God To Bless You?

Note: A question was asked by the Pastor unto His Students in The Lord, this is the question that was asked.

Message # 35   **Written in the year 2015.**

Greetings in The Wonderful Name of Jesus Christ; happy am I to be sharing with you another Wonderful Message Inspired by God. Looking at the question that was asked, I've Observed that there isn't one person in the whole world that can actually lift their hands and say that they do not need God's Blessing.

We must realize that this question is speaking to us personally, of what it truly means for us to receive God's Blessing.

Many people will openly say that this experience of Receiving God's Blessing, will; must; and is going to be great. But not many of us have come to the realization that when God puts His Hands on our lives whether to bless or to curse, it is a must, that our lives will never be the same, whether for good or evil.

It is easy to say with our mouth and desire with our heart of needing God's Blessing; but being able to fulfill The Requirements to first Receive The Blessing, and after that The Requirement to keep the same Blessing that you have Received is a Disciple only God Can Give. It is obviously seen that most of the Stories in The Bible are about People, Saints, and Servants of God, like ourselves that have all Received The Promise of their Blessing, and started off very well with The Blessing that God has Given them; But upon reading most of these Stories we realize that there strength began to fail; their eyes were no longer focused on God; They got too Comfortable and Relaxed with The Blessing, that they forgot that The Blessing Required a more harder work to Maintain The Blessing than to Receive The Blessing. Let me make this very clear, God The Giver of The Blessing is not at fault; all the blame rests on us The Saints of God, because we did not fully carry out all that is Required of us to ensure that we can keep the blessing.

One of the main challenge that we face as Children of God is that when we Receive The Blessing, and continue for a while to keep the Blessing; we forget that one of the most important Ingredient to Keep The Blessing is to make sure that we are Responsible enough to do what The Bible Ask us to do, which is to Teach our children and our children's children about God, so that our children can understand has we do, the main reason why we got The Blessing, and the importance of keeping The Blessing, to ensure that this same Blessing continues throughout the family lineage. Deuteronomy Chapter 6.

I realized that most people or Saints don't understand the importance of their Continuation; again let me say this, it is not how you start, because we need to remember that everyone essentially starts, but the big question is; how many of us actually finished the race. We are reminded in The Bible; many are called but only few are chosen.

Let's get back to the importance of the family lineage. We are reminded in The Scriptures which Says: They without us could not be made perfect. The person that at first Received the Blessing is the person that is known as the Foundation or the Beginner / Root of that same Blessing; everyone that continues under the same Rules and Guidelines of that same Blessing, are known as the Continuation of that Blessing, which are now the Branches that grows to produce the Fruits. This now allows the children of the main tree that got the Blessing to enjoy the same privileges of the Blessing, which are now the Fruits that this tree now begins to bear; the children not being the tree that made the initial Sacrifice to receive the Blessing, but doing their part to ensure that they keep the Rules and Commandment of God; this will ensure that the Blessing will be Maintained, and also Improve.

As children, our commitment to following The Commandments of God will ensure that our parent's Sacrifice and Blessing Received from God is not done in vain. That which our parents have done we could not have done, but that which we are now doing to stand on The Commandments of God, this ensures that our family's name remains in The Book of Blessing, The Covenant made between God our Forefathers and their children is not broken.

Our Continuation is important because when we have reached a state that we become older in God, we will need someone of our Lineage, who is younger and much stronger than us with the same principles that we have in God or even better principles, to stand up and ensure that our Covenant which we've made with God is not broken; hence The Blessing Remains with our Continuation.

Here is a cry commonly made:

"I Need God To Bless Me"!

Nothing is wrong with needing God to Bless us; but here is something that is needful for us to know. It is already God's Intention to Bless His Children, but what many of us don't know is that there are so many of us that are asking and begging and also pleading for God to Bless us, that we don't realize that the fault is in us why the process of blessing has not begun. First thing to know is that many of us are not Children to God's Will and Commandment; we pray the prayer often:

"Thy Will Be Done, Thy Kingdom Come".

But how many of us that are seeking God's Blessing are actually seeking with the same amount of energy, to do exactly what God asks us to fulfill. St. John Chapter 15:7. Says:

"If ye abide in Me, and My Words abide in you, you shall ask what you will and it shall be done".

Here is a Clue: Before we go to God, asking Him to Give us the World, make certain of one thing: (That we are Abiding in Him, and His Word can be found in us whenever time He Searches; to make sure that the Requirement is in place for us to Receive His Blessing).

Many of the things that God Asked us to Do in His Word, we haven't even started to look in the direction of doing it, much less to do it, but miraculously we need God to look beyond His Words of Requirement and Bless us. God and His Word are One, therefore if we are not keeping God's Word, it means that we are not Pleasing God, which means that we will never be in line to receive God's Divine Blessing. God's Divine Blessings is Reserved in Storage for those Saints who decide that they are going to Do What The Word of God Ask them to Do; because it's not the hearers who are justified but doers.

Many Saints reading this Message may be asking this question. Does God Only Seeks to Bless one Type of people? It depends on how you look on it, there are blessings in measurements and limits, and also Spiritual Blessings which last for a person's continuation, and these type of blessings are different and superior in measurement to that of physical blessings which is limited and are only measured to last for a limited time; there are many people that says, thank you God for waking me up this morning, of which they are right to declare that speech because for God to allow a person to see another day, it is truly a Blessing which must be acknowledged, But look at this; that same privilege that God gave us to see another morning is also granted to the man that just yesterday; killed, steal and rape; even to that man, that curse The Almighty God.

What's the difference you may ask: It is granted unto all mankind for life the access of God's Permitted Blessing. God's Blessing permits us to live and to receive the benefits that life has to offer, so is it with everyone else, because they too have this privilege to receive God's Permitted Blessing.

God's Divine Blessing is Positioned in The Hands of The Almighty God, Waiting for those who have come to the realization that they need to do exactly what The Word of God Says, by understanding what The Word of God Asked us to Do. And only God Alone Will Know when we are actually doing His Requirements. After God Is Satisfied that we are doing His Requirements, then we will realize the change in The Atmosphere of our lives because God's Divine Blessing will come upon us and overtake us. God's Word cannot lie, if we're not experiencing the Divine Blessing of God being a Christians, it simply means that something is wrong with our walk with God. This is not to declare that all saints will gain the access of God's Divine Blessing immediately, but to declare that if we are determined with our Christian walk then through Patience this type of walk will give birth into our existence.

The Characteristic for a person that is in God's Divine Blessing are:

1. **This person has Repented of their sin and Baptised in The Name of The Lord Jesus Christ.**
2. **This person has Received The Gift of The Holy Ghost.**
3. **This person's whole life must be, and is The Word of God, and not to hear but to Do The Word. Or potentially leading in that direction according to God's View and Time.**

4. This person's decision making privileges are now dead, this person only listens and does exactly what God Wants them to Do. This person has a Camel-like attitude.
5. This person completely TRUST In God.

One of the main thing I find people having a problem with is the word **REPENT**, which means having Godly sorrows for sin; meaning that we are completely sorry for all the sins we have committed, and we've now turned our backs from practicing all forms of sin, never to do them anymore, but now following in The Footsteps of God. And again we must identify that repentance is necessary but it is also patient.

In Genesis Chapter 12. The Story about God Making a Covenant promise with Abraham to bless him, and in his seed shall all the families of the earth be blessed. That Covenant Promised was completely dependent on Abraham's Obedience to God's Request. Not only was Abraham to obey God, but also he had to sacrifice leaving his family behind; yes, the family and relatives and all his associates that he grew up with and have known them for all his lifetime. Abraham was seventy-five (75) years old when God Gave him that Commandment; that's how long Abraham knew his family and companions.

How many of us would be willing to make a Sacrifice like that, and then travel to a place that you know nothing about. If there is one thing that Abraham's story taught me, is that in Receiving God's Blessing It Required Obedience; Trust and also to become knowledgeable that the Promise is for a specific time in the future for it to be fulfilled.

There are many of us that hear about God's Blessing and we would desire to receive that Blessing the same time or the very next day. The true reality is, that's not how it works; if God is going to work a miracle in our lives that's different, because miracles take place immediately, in the very same time it is Spoken out of The Mouth of God it Happens. But Blessing always has Conditions Applied to it and is always spoken for a particular time to come, but when it is Spoken, The Seed from God is Planted, providing that where the Seed is sent to resembles a **GOOD GROUND**.

There is another view to understand Blessing from God; this is it, one of the main reasons why Blessing takes a period of time to be fulfilled upon our life, is because it is mainly dependent upon the person that is receiving the Blessing. Why is this so you may ask: There is nothing impossible for God to do, but God Being Who He Already Is; Searches the Future and knows what the future holds for each and every one of us. Therefore, God Knows already that it is going to take Brother Blake approximately one (1) year to fulfill that which is Required by God to Do in order for him to receive his Blessing. On the other hand, God Sees that Brother Bentle will come to a quicker understanding towards His Requirements and begin to Do, therefore he will receive his Blessing in the period of three (3) months.

This is what I need for us to understand about this Message: It must be obvious by now; that all our Blessings which we should receive from God are all conditioned wrapped. And this is the condition, that we must first come to the full understanding of that which is required for us to receive our personal Blessing from God. There is a Blessing there for everyone who is a believer of Christ; therefore, No one needs to envy any one for their Blessing that they have received, because the only way a person could receive their Blessing is because they have done that which is Required by God.

Look at the Story with Cain and his Brother Abel; both of them had the access to give to God for the receiving of their Blessing, one did the Required Sacrifice, while the other did not do the Required Sacrifice; one brother's Sacrifice was Accepted, while the other was Rejected. Genesis Chapter 4:1-16.

Fact, the Children of Israel delayed their own Blessing because of disobedience and also they did not meet God's Requirement to establish that which should be Released by God. The story of the Children of Israel should teach us a lesson, that whenever we as children Disobey God; that act of Disobedience will delay our Blessings a great while, because we have not reached The Requirement that God needs us to reach.

God Has Brought to my understanding that one of the main reason why Abraham's Blessing took him twenty-five (25) years for him to receive it; was not only to show forth God's Great Power, but also to allow Abraham to reach his full requirement in God, which is complete belief in The Power of The Almighty God. Think about it, if God had not shown to Abraham that He WAS and still IS The Almighty God even in his old age; would Abraham have that confidence to go ahead and offer his only son Isacc for a Sacrifice, because The Bible says that (Abraham accounting that God was able to raise him up, even from the dead; from whence also he received him in a figure). Hebrews Chapter 11:19.

Therefore, we get to realize that the Requirement stage to receive his Blessing also prepared him to go through an even higher test to receive even Greater Blessings, only because Abraham was persistent in his soul to Obey The Will of The Almighty God. Every blessing has its Requirement; have we fulfilled God's Requirement for us to receive God's Blessing. The Bible says in Galatians Chapter 4:4.

"When the fullness of time was come, God sent forth his son, made of a woman, made under the law".

This Scripture brings evidence to us that everything that is to take place has a required time and season for it to happen.

Question to ask ourselves; am I one of those Saints that is only going to start well, and not able to finish the race?_____.
It is better for us to start slow and shaky, while giving ourselves a sure Foundation; and at the end receive the prize and cross the Finish line.

What does it mean for God to Bless me?_____.

The answer is Hard work, Dedication, Discipline, and don't forget the main ingredient which is Obedience. One of the most important gift in Christianity is the gift of Understanding; that when we receive it and start to Understand what is required, **We just do it.** True! It will take a little time to accept in order to fulfill, but The Spirit of God that Burns Continual Approval in our lives will create the Spiritual Appetite for a true Child of God to fulfill what God Needs for His Children to accomplish.

May God Continue to Bless and Keep you. I hope this Message will be a Blessing to you. From The Ministry of The Church of Jesus Christ Fellowship, Savannah Cross, May Pen, Clarendon, Jamaica, West Indies. Pastor Lerone Dinnall. God Bless You.

What Does It Mean For God To Bless ME?

The Only Saint That Have Obtained Their Blessing Are Those Who Believe That They Have Received Their Blessing.

Message # 1   **Date started April 26, 2016**
Date finished April 26, 2016.

Greetings and Salutations to all God's Wonderful and Blessed People. I can only Greet you in The Mighty Name of Jesus Christ, Our Soon Coming King. Believe me Saint of God; I was sitting in the Garden when I heard The Inspiration of this Message Came to me; and I had to immediately begin to write about this Message.

Identifying what The Message is talking about; we can clearly say that this is a continuation of The Message Faith that we were discussing, otherwise known as The Levels of Faith. This Message speaks towards identifying individuals, which have reached a level of Faith in God; that causes them to believe; that whatever their petition is from God, they are certain that God Has Already Granted them their hearts Desire. The Lord through this Topic Has Identified not all Saints, but a chosen few that have Evolved to another Level of Faith. Therefore, researching this Topic we will discover for ourselves the ingredients that make these few Saints different from the others, and try to replicate the success of their Faith to be our success of receiving our Blessing from God.

The only Saint that have Obtained their Blessings are those who Believe that they have Received their Blessing. What type of person is this?

_____.

Have a Look at these Seven Disciplines:

1. This person is **A Believer of The Lord Jesus Christ**; and have Baptized in His Name; this person has Received of The Holy Ghost; and fully believes that Jesus Christ died for our sins; that we may have life.

2. Another thing that we can identify about this individual, is that, this is a person that is **ABIDING IN THE WORD OF GOD**; which means that they live The Word; they Walk The Word; they Talk The Word of God; and you can go as far as to say that this person Sleep with The Word of God on His or Her Mind. The Bible Says:

"Not the Hearers are Justified; but the Doers".

3. The next thing that is clear to identify is that this is a person that is **PRAYING TO GOD**. This is a discipline that not a lot of people that are saints like to do, but this Message is Clearly demonstrating to us an example of what we should all aspire to become by developing A Personal Relationship with God; that we know that when we speak, our speech can be identified as one that Replicate that of **A SON OF GOD**; which will ensure that God Hears what we have spoken unto Him.

4. The next discipline will be identified in our prayers that there is found to be **No Iniquity** in our Conversation with our Father; also the practice must be established in our Lives, such as our Walking; in our Talking; and also in our Being. We must understand that God Is No Respecter of

Persons; He Will Not Take a person's right, and Give it to another person; whether they be righteous or unrighteous. The Lord's Judgement is done with **Equity**; meaning **Equal Rights**. Everyone that comes to God in Prayer; the first thing that God Does is to Put us on His Scale, to See if we do Measure exactly what we say we Measure. The Bible Says in Psalms 66:18.

"If I Regard Iniquity in my Heart, The Lord Will Not Hear Me".

This is where we Identify the different Obstacles that come in play, that prevents both our Prayers and our Faith to reach up to a Level that will Allow God to Release that which we Ask of Him.

5. Another Ingredient that comes into the mixture of this Saint is The Revelation of Love; especially **The Brotherly Love** that God Expects us to have.

6. The next Ingredient that is Evident; that must be apart of who we are; is A Discipline we have learnt in other Messages, which is a Decree for those who are Serving The Living God: Everything that we may ever Ask God for; **MUST; MUST; MUST; be in The WILL of GOD for it to even be considered to Be Answered by our Father**. If we can just read The Bible to follow in the FootSteps of God's Rule; then we will identify that, the moment we step out of God's Rule, this will bring the evidence as to why our Prayers Will Not Be Answered. I will remind my Readers of the words that says;

"THY WILL BE DONE; THY KINGDOM COME; IN EARTH HAS IT IS IN HEAVEN".

My Advice: If we need God to Answer our Prayers; then we must be Disciplined enough to Study His Word to make sure that all our Request is actually Fulfilling His Will. Anything that does not Replicate God's Will; that request Will Not Be Granted. It is no secret that many have fought for something that is outside of God's Will; of which the Manifestation of those things, we will have to live with, to bear the Consequences of that which we have pursued after. We will Observe many people uttering the lamentations of not waiting on God, when they realize, that which they have fought to receive; now becomes a Serpent, that Bites; and the Bite is very painful.

7. The next characteristic is revealed in a discipline to **WAIT IN GOD**; which in its explanation means to **REST IN GOD**. Saints; this is where we find our weakness. Not a lot of us; are willing to Wait In God; for some strange reason we believe that, if we are doing the work ourselves, it will be completed at a quicker time. There is a saying that goes like this:

"God Is Slow but He Is Sure".

It depends on how we look at it: For me; My God Is Never Slow; because if He Is Slow that means that I am Dead; because He Won't Be Able to reach me on time when my enemy does attack me. God Does Things in His Time; and we have got to believe that while we are in our Waiting Season; God Is Not Going to Allow Anything to Happen to us. There is nothing anyone can do to cause God to Change His Time that He Has Set. The Bible encourages us to wait on The Lord; be of good courage, and He Will Strengthen our hearts. Those that Wait upon The Lord shall renew their strength; they shall mount up with wings as Eagles; they shall run, and not be weary; they shall walk, and not faint.

Question to all of us that are reading this Message: Have we Reached The Level of Faith; that this Topic is speaking of; that will allow us to believe that we have already Received? Are all these seven Characteristics that have been listed; are they a part of the Ingredients that make up who we are before God?

_____.

We've got to understand that even if we say yes; there is A God that Says:

"SHALL NOT I SEARCH IT OUT".

My Advice: Let us seek to measure up to God's Expectation; because we must realize by now that **God Is A Dictator**; it must be His Way or no way at all for those who are His Children.

I hope that you have enjoyed this Message; let us all seek to help each other to make it into God's Kingdom. May The Favor of God Continue to be upon your lives; God Bless. From the Servant of God; Your Brother; Your Friend; Your Minister and Pastor Lerone Dinnall.

Receive Your Blessing By Faith In The Name Of The Lord Jesus Christ.

Understanding The Balance Of Life...

Message # 38   **Date Started November 15, 2016**
                                     Date Finalized December 2, 2016.

I Will Bless The Lord at all times, His Praise shall continually be in my mouth. I greet all My Father's Children in The Wonderful Name of our Soon Coming King Jesus Christ; I count this another opportunity to write A Message Inspired by GOD as a Privilege, Honour and a Blessing.

The truth is, these Messages are changing lives, and are allowing Christians to have a firm grip to God, by allowing them to see things clearer; these Messages are allowing those who are not yet Saved, to be drawing closer to the possibilities that they must now be in a Mind frame that they must be Saved. And for this I am extremely Joyful and Blessed; there are many people that will never give a helping hand to someone in need, except that person is able to help them in another way that will be of benefit to them. But that is not The Mission that God Called us to Perform; God Called us as Believer to simple become The Light of the World that others will see The Glory of God in us, that God Will Then Allow His Glory to be Transformed in them by the Conviction of The Word of God.

There is no possible way that God Will Be Comfortable for those who are His Servants to established a position that they now have become the center of attraction to Receive of God's Glory; The Bible Said My Glory Will I Not Give to another, therefore, If we are members of Christ and have not yet understand the Position of our Existence then it's simple, we have not yet understood the Purpose of our Christian lives in God.

Let me share something with you: For years I've been in Church, before I was Called by God to Build an Altar for Him; looking at the Examples of those who are set over me to perform as Instructors, seeking to pattern what they would esteem as being A Christ Like lifestyle, and also determined to make sure that my mark was also made in this life for Christ; and for years I've been doing what I thought would be Pleasing in The Eyes Of GOD, until one day when I felt burnt out by doing these duties, I consulted The Lord by asking why is it that there seems to be no end to these duties, why are these duties so heavy to carry out, and why is it that I am now in a position that I feel like I can no longer manage the Responsibilities of what I'm doing for God. The Lord Response to me was:

"Who Told You To Do All These Duties"!

Then it was there that I suddenly began to realize that I never got an OK from The Voice of God pertaining to these duties, these duties were not mine to fulfill, they were the duties of other members that were assigned to fulfill these tasks.

Can you imagine being in a Church, let's say for ten (10) years, and for that ten years you've not been fulfilling The Purpose of that which God Ask us to fulfill; what a **SHOCKER!** That means our whole purpose of being a Christian would now be of no value or meaning, because our purpose is not being fulfilled.

Note: It is important being Children of God to make certain that we are indeed following The Instructions of God by the Conformation that whatever is asked of us to do, is actually what God Requires us to Do at our Level that we are at. Yes, there are Levels in Christianity; that when we passed one level, we can no more go back to be doing the things that we did in the previous level;

and then many People or Saints will look on us and think that we are being scornful, which is true, but I don't think scornful is the word to used; it is more a word that is called **TERRIFIED, HORRIFIELD and SCARED**; because once we have Elevated in God, and begin to see things in The Spiritual, there is no way we are going to give any opportunity for the devil to draw us back down from The Level that God Has Now Placed us; the Truth is, we have Elevated from Level one of Holiness to Level two, and now having the ambition to elevate to Level three and beyond.

Question: Why do you think the devil is Angry when A Child of God has reach A Level that they begin to Elevate from one Level of Holiness to another?_____. He is Angry because he has lost one more soul that was under the guidance of the influence of this World, to now being under The Influence of The Almighty God. And that one Soul can change a thousand more Souls; less people going to hell, and more on the pathway for Heaven. After realizing God's Answer to me, It was then I made a Conscious Decision that I will not be performing duties that are outside of my portfolio.

Can you just imagine being the owner of a Restaurant; one day you came to your business and observe that the Head Chef is cleaning the windows and parking the cars for customers, and then realize that the person who is destined to perform those tasks is now in the Kitchen preparing the meal for the Prime Minister. What am I saying! This is what I'm saying; let us know our purpose that God Needs us to Perform Being His Servants, because we will spend years doing a duty that was not fit for us to accomplish. The Bible Declares in St Matthew Chapter 7:21-23.

> **"Not everyone that saith unto Me, Lord, Lord, shall enter into The Kingdom of Heaven; but he that doeth The Will of My Father which is in Heaven. Many will say to me in that day, Lord, Lord, have we not prophesied in Thy Name? And in**

Thy Name have cast out devils? And in Thy Name done many wonderful works? And then Will I Profess unto them, I Never Knew You: Depart from Me, ye that work Iniquity".

Let us not seek to find out on that day that the duties we are performing for God is actually not our Mission to fulfill; let us rather be desirous only to Do The Will of God. God Promised that if we come unto Him, all those who labour and are heavy laden, then He Will Give Us Rest. The Lord Said that His Yoke Is Easy, and His Burden Is Light. St Matthew Chapter 11:28-30.

- Here is a Question: Since becoming A Christian, are we still burdened with loads?

  _____.

- Are we still laboring to obtain **THE CARROT OF PROMISES** that will never be achieved?_____.

If our answer is yes, then it simply means that we have not yet found our **REST IN GOD**.

There is Physical Evidence that is there to allow us to understand more about positions in which we labour.

- Can a man whose weight is 100 pounds fit in the clothes of a man whose weight is 200 pounds?_____.
- Can a man who wears a size 7 shoes, can he now be comfortable in a size 10 or even smaller, a size 6 shoes, the answer is no; likewise The Spiritual Things of God, someone who has been Trained by God for years, there is no way someone who has no training will be able to accomplish the task that God Has Destined for that person which was Trained, that God Has Prepared for that man to Accomplish; one man will be fully wearing The

Armour of God, while the other would not be wearing God's Protection.

For the man that God Has Prepared, these duties will be nothing to Accomplish, walking over Principalities and Powers, Spiritual Wickedness in High places, the Elements and the Environment and Forces of the Devil; it would be like walking on water, of which a normal man who is not yet Trained and Born Again, this person will not be able to Accomplish God's Mission. Truth be told friends, God Has Some Simple Duties that He Has Asked some of us to Accomplish, of which many of the times we ignore and seek to do those duties of which we were not called to Accomplish.

I recalled Bishop Austin Whitfield said that he gave a Testimony one day, when he just got saved; and he Testified Saying:

**"I had rather be a doorkeeper in The House of My God, than to dwell in the tents of wickedness".
Psalms 84:10**

This simple duty The Lord Allowed him to fulfill for years by being A Deacon in God's House, then Elevated him to become an Elder, then an Overseer, then to The Office of A Bishop. The example of this Testimony prove that we have got to find ourselves in the position that we can perform the little that God Ask us to Perform, before we can be Elevated to perform the Major things that we will now be Trained to Performed for God; because it is the Small Duties that allow us to be able to have The Experience to Manage the Big Duties.

Are we called to be A Door Keeper? Let us become the best Door Keeper The Lord Has Ever Seen. Called to be a brother or a Sister; called to be a Deacon or a Minister; called to be an Evangelist or a Missionary; called to be an Overseer or A Pastor; called to be a Prophet or a Bishop, let us seek to take each Duty as a Major priority before GOD and man. And then there is a Duty that God Has Called all of us to Fulfill, and that is to just be An Example for Him and live for God.

There is a Topic given that must be explored, Namely, Understanding The Balance of Life. I speak the truth, except it was The Spirit of God that Explained this Topic, I don't think I would have completely understood what this Topic is saying. To understand The Balance of Life, we have got to first seek to understand The Purpose of this same life that we live each day.

THE PURPOSE OF LIFE...

This is not to please ourselves by doing what we feel like doing for ourselves; and also it is not to please others. The purpose of life is rather to identify and be born in the knowledge that our very Existence was made for the sole purpose being only to please and to fulfill what God would have us to accomplish. This fact is a discovery that many of us as Saints take a very long time to accept; and the longer it takes us to accept the conclusion of this belief, the longer it is going to allow us to walk in the True Purpose of what God Called us to Accomplish in this life. I'm sure that we are familiar with these words:

"I AM MY OWN PERSON, I CAN DO WHAT I FEEL LIKE DOING, WHENEVER I FEEL LIKE DOING IT"!

This Mind set and forceful attitude in the wrong direction is a spirit that must be killed, if it is that we are truly desirous to understand and to accept what is the true purpose of our existence.

- Let us ask ourselves this Question: Can that which is created by **THE CREATOR** have an opinion as to the purpose of that which it is created to fulfill?

  _____.

- Let's put it another way: Can the sun and the moon say to God that Created them, that they will no longer give forth their light in the time that they are called to do their jobs?

  _____.

- Can the fish of the sea make a decision by no longer swimming in the sea, but now choose to walk on the dry land?_____.

Therefore, So is it with us as human beings, we were Created and called for the only purpose, that being, to be of Service to The King of kings and The Lord of lords.

And if it is that we find ourselves not being of Service to God, then I would have us to remember the story of the Fig Tree, although it was not the time for the fruit of Figs according to The Bible; this Fig Tree found itself in a position, that when The Master called, the Tree was not in **A Ready State** to answer The Master's Request; we are also reminded of the Parable with the five Wise Virgins and the five Foolish Virgins, The Bible Declared that they both received the Message to be ready for the Marriage because The Bride Groom Cometh. After making themselves ready to the best of their ability, according to the Level of their own Understanding, the Call for the Marriage took place at Midnight, when everyone should be sleeping and was sleeping. Think about it, when The Lord Request for us to Accomplish that which God Ask us to fulfill, does God Cares that it's now dark, at the time of "3 AM" in the morning and it is the period that ManKind will be sleeping, does that stop God from Making His Request Be Made Known?_____.

Here is a Question that is important to ask ourselves:

"AM I BEING OF SERVICE FOR GOD"?

_____.

If that answer is not yes, then it is time for us to examine ourselves to identify who it is that we are being of Service to. Is it ourselves, or a man or a woman, is it for our Parents, Ministers, Missionaries or Pastors and Bishop? Because if God Is Not Being Pleased by The Offerings that comes from us, then how is it that we are on our way to Heaven!

The last time we stepped into The House of God, did God Receive His Glory from The Offerings that we Gave to Him?

_____.

The last time we encouraged someone, did they leave the conversation by acknowledging that God Is Great and Worthy to be Praised; or did they tell us how great the conversation with them was, by letting us feel like we are that person that Performed the Miracle that took place in that very conversation?

_____.

I cannot emphasize enough, we have got to be very careful that whatever we are doing for God, stays in the category of remaining for God's Glory. Let us work for God, and not for ourselves; after the work is done, remember to say:

"To God Be The Glory, Great Things He Had Done".

Jesus Christ Being God in the Flesh was very careful of receiving Glory that came to Him, because being in Flesh He did not count Himself Worthy to accept Glory, seeing that the time for him to be Glorified was not yet come. You would often hear Jesus Christ after Performing a Miracle asking the recipients of these Miracles to Give to God The Glory; there was one time He asked the blind man that he had Healed, if he knew what the Offering that must be given to

The Lord House was, and He Told him to Go forth and Give to The House of The Lord that which Was Required by The Law of God.

It is recorded in The Bible, every occasion The Lord Jesus Christ cast out demons, He suffered them not to speak, because they knew that He Was The Lamb of God, that cometh to Die for the Sin of the World. The Lord Being in the form of Flesh could not be side tracked from Doing what was Destined for Him to fulfill, therefore, Being in the flesh to fulfill A Purpose, He Stayed Away from Being Praised, Honored and Glorified by men; except at the time when it was to be fulfilled by Scripture at the Triumphant entry into Jerusalem, when all the people cried:

"Hosanna to The Son of David: Blessed Is He That Cometh in The Name of The Lord; Hosanna in The Highest". St Matthew Chapter 21:9.

At that particular time the Chief Priest and the Scribes murmured, and it is mentioned in The Book of St Luke Chapter 19:39. That the Pharisees asked Jesus Christ to Rebuke His Disciples, because of the Glory and the Praise that uttered from their Lips along with the other people. The Lord Response Was:

"I Tell you that, if these should hold their peace, the stones would immediately cry out".

Therefore, Making known to us that the Season of time was now manifested, that Jesus Christ should and must be Glorified by the mouth of men. Therefore, The Purpose of life is concluded in the words that is known as **SERVICE FOR GOD.** If we are not willing to Offer Service to God and for God, don't worry, someone else will be more than joyful to accept the Responsibilities to Serve God, even if it takes them to be awake at "3 AM" in the Morning to Fulfill What God Asked them to Do.

THE BALANCE OF LIFE...

It is important to identify that the life we are speaking about is that of a person that Is Born of God and only for this existing life. Therefore, A person that has not yet been Born Spiritually may not understand or even come into the agreement that this is true. Life Is A Balance of two parts, just like everything else in this life exists by two completely different Characteristics. It is identified that there is The Supreme Existence of The Almighty God, and the opposite of God's Manifestation is the fact that there is a devil the hater of everything that is good. There is life and there is death; there is light and there is darkness; there are higher grounds, also can be identified as Higher Levels In God, and there are the plains, which can also be considered as Lower Levels In God. There Is Heaven and there is hell, there is Good and there is bad. Life is like a Scale with two Measuring Balances, one Balance which is Physical is completely linked to the Spiritual life which is Superior and is first to that of the Physical Life, while the other Balance is completely manifested in The Spiritual life and linked directly to the Physical life.

The difference however with this Scale, is that The Spiritual Balance has The Higher Authority, which contributes to what happens to the Balance that is in the Physical life. Therefore, through Visions, The Lord Identifies that a Man's Spiritual life is of Greater Importance than that of a Man's Physical life. It is Revealed that the Spiritual Scale Blessings / Weights is Given only to teach us how to walk in the Physical life, to be able to know exactly how to Please God and thus enabling us to reach the Requirement desired by The Spiritual Life to make it into Heaven.

Whatever we perform in the Physical Life even if it causes us to die earlier than the expected time, as long as it is a Requirement from God for us to Stand and to Uphold that which God Need for us to uphold, then in the Spiritual Life we would have reached **A**

Qualified State to enable us to be Worthy to receive all that Heaven has to Offer.

Therefore, When we look at it as a whole, we will discover that this Physical Life is but just A Training Ground to lead us in the life that lasts for **ETERNITY**. Therefore, Whatever we lose along the way of this journey, let us not pay it too much attention, because after every Cleansing of Material Object / Idols, there is then **A Revelation of God's Divine Blessing / Purpose for Our Life.**

The Lord Reveals that through The Balance of Life, whenever Promotions or Elevations should take place, this only happens in The Spiritual Scale first, then once the Scale Has Received; and we should all make a note on the word **RECEIVED**, because many Spiritual Permission is Granted, but God's People have not yet come to the realization that they have not Received The Blessing Spiritually, therefore, The Blessing is not Manifesting in the lives of God's People. The Blessing Is Already Declared, but it will only be Decreed when God's People have Accepted / Received the Permission to walk into A New Anointing.

Let's get back to The Revelation; when the Spiritual Scale Have Received this New Anointing, it then allows the Physical Scale to manifest what has already been done in The Spiritual Scale.

This Spiritual Scale Children of God is our Minds, and that is the biggest part of our lives that God Has Trouble with; because there is found in some of us, our Minds have been broken from a tender age, for others our Minds are Clouded by Powers and Principalities, Wicked devices and Demonic forces, Powers that would rather to keep us trapped, and in doubt that brings forth fear, which prevents us from believing what God Has Already Declared over our lives to be our **Decreed Deliverance.**

I saw something that took place before my very eyes; a person came to Church for healing, and said that they have received and accept the healing they desired by walking up and down in the Church and declaring to the members that I am healed; then after

Church has come to an end, this person then desires to visit the Doctor because their believe is that something may still be wrong that probably in their Mind, God Did Not or Could Not Heal. Now when you observe something like that, what can you say by this action; if my Mind was not focused on God, I would believe that there are chains holding down The Abilities of my God. What do you think?

Let's get back to the Visions, The Lord Also Reveals that The Spiritual Scale's weight or Blessings is for Everlasting, which means that God Will Not Take Back that which He Has Pronouns or Declared to be our Blessings; it is considered **FIXED**, even if, we have not yet come into the realization that it is Declared to be Decreed over our lives. Fixed in The Spiritual Scale, but still endures challenges in the Physical Scale for it to be Manifested or Decreed. This means that, many times there is Spiritual Approval Granted, but the Physical part of a man's life, which is his actions is plagued with Limits, because of his **BELIEF**. His Mind is not yet to the requirement to walk in that manifestation of The Spiritual; and some of the times it takes months and years for a person to make the breakthrough in order to walk in The Spiritual Blessing.

I would not be doing my job if I did not tell you the secret of how to fast track the breakthrough from The Spiritual Scale to The Physical Scale. There is a song writer that brought forth a song that Says:

> **"Away, away from the noise, alone with You;**
> **away, away to hear Your Voice, be with You".**

That's My Recommendation, there comes a time in our lives called a **CROSS ROAD**, that God Needs to Take us to another Level, because we've just outgrown the Level of which we are at now; a desire for A New and Fresh Anointing that cannot be given if you stand still or remain in the same position, but it is identified that every New Level and Glory from God must be Declared with the Action of **SEPARATION WHICH IS HOLINESS.**

There is a lot of things we desire and hold fast to, which we believe are necessary to have and to make sure we maintain, but can I tell you that most of what we hold unto in this life are completely Irrelevant to The Eternal Life, and to The Higher Level that God Needs us to Achieve. One of the main thing that stops us from Receiving / Obtaining what is Declared in the Spiritual Scale, is a Fact, we are just too Heavy; and God Needs us to let go of these Idols, that we can become light weight, thus enabling us to walk in Holiness, obtaining A New and Fresh Anointing from God.

Have you ever been in a position that those around you are telling you what God Is Saying and what God Wants or Needs you to Do, but still even though there are many to say what God would Desire of you to Do, there is still not the Conformation within your very soul that God Has Spoken to you to bring to light The Manifestation of His Will for your Life.

Learn this: People or other saints should not control our lives, it should be God, The Creator of Everything, GOD Has Complete Authority over our Lives. Many of us believe that Christianity is a Burden, because of the many Requirements that we are called to perform by man and not necessarily by God; then we find ourselves becoming burnt out and full of load, some of us lose our Minds. Have we ever Prayed this Prayer before God:

LORD, WHAT WOULD THOU HAVE ME TO DO?

It is Simple, but very Effective. It is then observed that after we have prayed this Prayer we identify that God's Answer for His Requirement upon our Lives Is Simple, without any Burdens, God Says:

"Make Your Life Shine For Me, Be Different, Be The Light Of God".

There are many people that will look on us as Christians being different as a crime; and may want you to conform to what everyone else is doing, just because they are doing what they are doing and are comfortable, which may not be in The Will of God. I can just hear them saying:

Why can't you be more like Sister Mary and Brother John.

When the truth is that God Has Imparted an Anointing upon your Life that you just cannot be like anyone else. This is not to say that Sister Mary and Brother John are not living for God, but this is to say and to establish that there are different levels and manifestations to being Light.

Some Light has different strength or brightness than others; some light are at a level, that if it is ever Introduce to a light of higher brightness, it would make or bring forth a feeling of jealousy, because that lesser light would have then discovered that there is A Greater Revelation and Manifestation of light that He or She have not yet begun to walk into.

Therefore, Being Light / Children of God, is not a word that comes with being Baptized, or being filled with The Holy Ghost, or even going to Church regularly. But having now become The Light of God, it is a combination of all these Requirements, along with meaningful Fasting, reading to understand The Word of God; which now brings forth our duty which is to maintain and to sharpen The Relationship with God that brings forth The Revelation of The Light of God in our lives, thus enabling us to climb through the Levels of the Manifestations and Brightness of being The Light of God.

I seek to remain a Humble Servant of God, also I seek to continue to be an Inspiration by The Will and Manifestation of God, to my fellow Brothers and Sisters in The Lord, I hope that this Message has been Seasoned with Grace for your life; let us seek to keep on Improving in The Will of God, because The Goal Is Heaven, and nothing less. I also ask that if you know of someone in need of A Word from God, don't be afraid to share The Word of God with a Soul that may be dying to hear A Word from God by your speech, that person will always remember that you took time out to ensure that they heard A Word from God, and if that person makes it into Heaven, that will be one Star in your crown.

Let us seek to change lives; the World is already taking away lives and condemning Souls to hell; let us be the difference maker with The Word of God. Marriages Can Be Saved; Sisters and Brothers can remain in Church; Sinners can be Converted in The Mighty Name of Jesus Christ.

In closing I repeat these words:

**"I WILL BLESS THE LORD AT ALL TIMES,
HIS PRAISE SHALL CONTINUALLY
BE IN MY MOUTH, AMEN".**

Pastor Lerone Dinnall.

Understanding
The Balance Of Life...

Now that I am Saved;
What Is God's
Expectation for my Life?

Message # 6   **Done in the Year 2015**.

I have read of The Call from the beginning through The Scriptures, I'm reading of it now, and it is a confirmation because I've read it in The Book of Revelation, that also in the future The Call shall be Holy, Holy, Holy, Is The Lord God Almighty, Which Was, and Is, and Is to Come.

I Greet all my Fathers Children in The Wonderful Name of Jesus Christ Our Soon Coming King. Happy am I to be writing for you another Wonderful Message Inspired by The True and Living Spirit of God.

I was basically Pushed to write A Message of this content, not that I wouldn't want to write a Message like this, but had to write this Message because I saw that many of us as Children of God do not know what exactly is Require of us by God to Be, and what to Perform. God Has Placed me in a position that I must be a Soul Protector, and not a person that sees something is about to happen and does nothing about it. Because The Bible Said that if the Watchman sees the sword, and warns not the people, it is on the Watchman's shoulders. Ezekiel Chapter 3.

Now this Topic is geared towards opening the eyes of God's People so that we will realize what God's Expectation is, now that we are Saved. And being Saved is a word that not many people understand; some people believe that being saved is an action done by water Baptism; or is an action that I'm going to Church often; or is an action that brings forth the Character that I have Repented of my Sin; or that I'm reading the Bible often; or that I love my neighbour as myself; or is it that I come to Prayer meeting whenever there is a prayer meeting; or is it that I'm always in a Fasting service; Or is it that I Heal the sick, Raise the dead or even cast out demons; or is it that I've receive The Gift of The Holy Ghost; or is it that I've received of all The Gifts of The Spirit?_____.

The Lord Revealed to me that I may Understand to look into the word that is called **"Now"**; when The People of God have come to the realization and expectation of the requirement that is necessary to allow us to be granted the Status of being Saved; they will realize that being Saved is an inward or Spiritual experience that has all the requirements that was before listed in the previous paragraph combined; and that none of these activity stands on its own feet, as they together resemble a body of what it takes to actually be a **"NOW SAVED"**.

There are many people that are in the **NOW** of their life, that believes that to be Saved brings forth the evidence that they are the best Singer on the choir, or that they are the best dressed servant in the congregation, or it is that they are the best Preacher or Teacher the world Have ever seen; or it is that we give Tithes and Offering better than anyone else. Many of us are also of the belief that the person that has the most money is an excuse or a sign to show who it is that is more Saved. The word belief is a strong word, that brings forth a strong attitude from that person that believe in whatsoever he or she believes in; there is nothing wrong with believing, but we've got to make sure that whatsoever we believe in, actually comes from God, which means that it has foundation and continuation that reflects The Three Views of God being Past, Present and Future, which Stands Firm and is Spiritually Tied into The Authority of God; and we must all know by now that everything that has foundation comes from

God, which reflects a sure continuation of that foundation, therefore it cannot be moved.

That which comes from God Will Always have fight and opposition, because we've got to realize that The Word of The Lord Is Tried has Gold that goes through the fire to ensure that it is really gold; so is The Word of The Lord Tried to ensure that it is indeed The Lord that had Spoken that Word in your life. We must remember The Word of The Lord that Said:

"Upon this ROCK I Will Build My Church and the gates of hell shall not prevail against it". St Matthew Chapter 16:13-19.

Do you know what The Rock Is?_____.

The Rock Is The WORD of GOD that demonstrates that Salvation only comes through The Power of Jesus Christ; Therefore, Whoever is building on The Word of God through the access of Jesus Christ, which means you believe in The Word of God and is doing what The Word ask you to do, by the command of what The Lord Tells you to Do; it is certain, that individual cannot fail because God Cannot Fail. When we believe in The Word of God and are doing what The Word asks us to Do; it doesn't matter if we are the only people that believe, and the whole world is against us; it is certain, because we are Standing on God's Word, we will never be Defeated. If The Word of God is in us, that means that God's Kingdom is Being Built in us.

I happen to be looking on the word Saved; and seeking to understand what it will really take for a person to be Saved; The Lord Opened my eyes to see a little deeper to understand that being Saved is not one activity that stands by itself, but rather it is a cooperative body of function and purposes that comes together to enable a Believer to actually be Saved. Many of these functions and purposes take a long time in most of our lives for us to actually Develop and be made perfect in our lives. But looking on the word **SAVED**, The Lord Revealed this to me:

"Being SAVED Is Being Sanctified; Being Anointed; Being Victorious; Being Effective; and Being Delivered from Sin".

S = Sanctified
A = Anointed
V = Victorious
E = Effective
D = Delivered From Sin

All the meanings of these words combined enable us to be truly **SAVED** according to God's Standard. Now man's standards and interpretation may be different; but God's Standard is what He Says it is. Now upon looking at these words, when we examine ourselves, are we truly Saved, or is there still a lot of work that needs to be done in us to accomplish the process of being Saved?_____.

To become A Child of God Requires of us to be Trained, if we are not willing to be Trained then we won't be able to be a Good Servant; one of the best ways to be Trained is to read and put into practice that which The Word Ask of us to Do.

Let's take a closer look on these words:

- **Sanctified:** Set apart from those things that are not of God's Will; also means to make Holy, Consecrated, to be Purified or free from Sin.
- **Anointed:** To be Consecrated in order to be used by God for special purposes and extraordinary missions, that only the person that is anointed can carry out.
- **Victorious:** Whatever God sends you forth to Do, because you have been Obedient to His Call to be Sanctify and have

been Anointed; therefore, whatsoever you do according to His Will, in The Name of Jesus Christ, you will always be Victorious.

- **Effective:** We are the Salt of the earth, We are a city that is set upon a hill that cannot be hid; God Goes before us, God Goes behind us, and more important, God Is In us; therefore, Whatever we put our hands to, it must be Decreed for the purpose that it is set out for, by the laying of our hands and the speech of our mouth. We've now Become A Son of God; not everyone is A Son of God, there are a lot of people that are in the process of becoming Sons of God, but they are not there yet; they are still Believers to become Sons of God.

- **Delivered From Sin:** Sins are Spiritual baggage, a Child of God will never be able to walk into Spiritual Approvals with spiritual burdens still being attached to them. A Child of God must always remember that their greatest defence against sin is to make certain that they confess their sins before God First, failure to do this will result in that sin now being birth to become unconfessed sin and unforgiven sin; these will always cripple and create a permanent crack in the vessel of any Child of God, thus we are made and remain not effective for The Call of Saving Grace.

Serving God to become Sons of God, we must realize that we have to graduate from the Basic School of knowing about God, and get to the Primary level of knowing about God; then Graduate from the Primary School, to elevate to the High School level of knowing about God; then graduate from the High School level and elevate to the College level of knowing about God; then graduate from College level, and elevate to the University level of knowing about God, and graduate from the University level of knowing about God to be born into The Heaven's Language and Revelation of knowing about God;

and if there is any other levels, then we must try our very best to elevate to that level because in God we can never stop learning about how Great and how Wonderful He Truly His.

The problem with those of us that are seeking God is that we settle too often, and sometimes the level that we are settling at is not the level that God wants us to settle; that's if there is even a desire in God for us to settle. This is what we say many times.

I know this about God, there is no need for me to know anything else!

God Always Requires His Children to know more and continue the journey to Know even more for our lives about God than that which we expect to know. We are the Individual that decides to Settle at whatever level we are in God.

The Foundation for the expectation for our lives in God is surrounded by this Scripture that is found in The Book of Leviticus Chapter 11:44-45. And 1 Peter Chapter 1:13-16. Which gives God's People a General / Foundational Commandment of God's Expectation for all those who desire to Become Sons of God. This is what The Word Says:

"Be ye Holy; for I Am Holy".

We must realize by now that God's Expectation for us as followers is for us to become **SAVED**; and only then after we've become Saved can we be truly numbered as one that is Called and Chosen to Become Sons of God.

Therefore, The Expectation is and always was, whether we know it or not, It is The Standard for us to become **SONS OF GOD**. Now after realizing this Fact, let me say like Brother Paul:

"Shall we continue in Sin that Grace may abound; God forbid".

Which means God Says No. Romans Chapter 6:1-14. Must I continue to be the Old Person I was! Or should I seek to become what is God's Expectation for my life, which is The New Man?

_____.

Is there any merit in continuing to be of that old character; if there is, why then did we make the move from Sin to Life?

_____.

Think about it; It can never be God's Will that I keep the same friends that I am accustomed to keep; It definitely cannot be alright for the old life and old behaviour to come over and to be a part of this New Life and New Behaviour.

I would like to draw your attention to a Story in The Bible, where people thought it was ok to bring over the old behavior into A New Life with God. Acts Chapter 5:1-11. These two Saint of God sold a property that was theirs, and brought only a part of the money; now it was ok if they wanted to give only a part of the money but they decided to lie, and said to The Man of God Peter, that what they had brought was actually what they sold the land for. This couple didn't just tell the Servant of God a lie, they actually told that lie before The Face and Presence of God.

This they did, and the consequence of their Sin was death. This old character was the old man of lies, which when we come to God, He Needs us to demand for this Old man to remain being buried or else.

Another example of the Old Man being brought in the New Life can be found in the Book of Joshua Chapter 7. This Old Man that was demonstrated had a characteristic of being disobedient to God's Commandment. The Command was given that they should kill all their enemies and to destroy everything that belongs to their enemies; but there was a man by the name of Achan that Disobeyed the Commandment of God; he took a Babylonian garment; he stole silvers and gold, and hide it under his tent in The Assembly of God's People. What this activity caused is for not only Achan to be under Sin in God's Eye; but for his entire household; his entire tribe and also for the entire nation of Israel to be guilty of Sin even though only one man knew what he did.

The Lord Allowed me to Realize through this story that whatever Sin we Bury or Hide, it actually grows and develops into a greater Sin than the one which we have committed. This story made me realize that many things can be going wrong in our lives and we are not directly at fault, but because someone who is in direct relationship to us has sin, it causes The Anger and Wrath of God to be over our lives.

The Bible Said that the Israelites could not look their enemies in the face, and that their hearts melted and became as water, having no courage to fight. What was more important about this Message was the reconciliation; The Children of Israel had to Sanctify themselves; and after Sanctification was done they had to Separate themselves from whatever that caused them not to be Sanctified in The Eyes of God.

The story revealed that they found out who had done wrong by not Obeying The Commandments of God; when they found him, they had to get rid of him; his wife; his children; his oxen; his asses; his sheep; his tent and all that he had; they stone them all and burned them with fire to make sure that they were completely destroyed. This they had to do because God's Favor was no longer on their side for them to be Victorious.

There are many of us that want to remain Saved, but we are just not willing to do the **SEPARATION** that God Requires of us to Do. Being A Child of God, there must always be in us a Willingness to do whatever God needs us to Do in order for us to be and remain a Son of God. If there is no separation in our lives for God, there can be no Relationship with God; that's how important separation is to God.

The Bible would further make us realize the importance of obeying God's Word when it Says in The Book of St Matthew Chapter 5:29-30.

"If thy right eye or right hand offend thee, we must cut it off".

This spoke Jesus Christ to confirm the importance to us of how serious it is for us to Do God's Requirements that we can enter The Kingdom of Heaven. When God Spoke those words, He meant it; both Spiritually and Physically. We must realize that The Lord Said **RIGHT** Eye and **RIGHT** Hand; He Was Speaking of whatever there is that is in our lives that is most dependable, and strongest source to our survival, meaning Strength; If it is that we've found out that, that which is the Strongest and most Dependable is going to prevent us from making it into God's Kingdom, whether Spiritual or Physical, we must get rid of it. Because it is better for us to enter The Kingdom of Heaven with one eye and one hand, than not to be entering at all.

This is the big Question: How many of us are truly willing to do all that it takes for us to ensure that we Please God; that His Favors Remain upon our lives?

What if our Husband and Wife is preventing us; it may be our children; or that friend that we grew up with; whatever it is, God needs us to be ready for **SEPARATION** that will lead to Recommitment to God's Will.

God Is Searching all over this World for Servants who are willing to Serve, meaning to do whatever they are Asked to Do. After we've become good Servants, we will now graduate to Become Sons of God. May God Continue to Bless you, as we seek to Train our lives together to Pattern The Complete Will of God.

Holy, Holy, Holy, Is The Lord God Almighty, Which Was, And Is, and Is to Come. From the Servant of God, Pastor Lerone Dinnall.

Let Us Walk In God's Expectation.

Becoming A Philip?

Message # 93
Date Started May 1, 2018
Date Finalized May 1, 2018.

I Give all Glory, Honor and Praise to The Only Living God, Jesus Christ, The King of kings and The Lord of all lords. I greet the entire Family of God in none other Name but The Name of Jesus Christ; privileged am I to be found in this Atmosphere that I'm called to write what Saith The Lord.

A lot of Souls are dying and are being led in the wrong direction of life, for the main reason because many that are called and Assigned the Responsibility to be and become gatekeepers for the Souls of man have Miserable Failed. I'm making note of and opening our eyes to the spirit of Pride that has been given license over our lives to manifest within the lives of Christians to believe that they have become more important than the cause and purpose of Christianity. We've become so Impossible that we forget that The Bible Said:

St Matthew Chapter 18:3-5.

"And he said, verily I say unto you, Except ye be converted, and become as little children, ye shall not enter into The Kingdom of Heaven. Whosoever therefore shall humble himself as this little child, the same is Greatest in The Kingdom

of Heaven. And whoso shall receive one such little child in My Name Receiveth Me".

I've discovered for myself that for most of us that are Serving God, if we are to help a Soul to turn their lives over to God, it would mean that such a person must be chained in the direction of The Ministry that we are a part of; if this person is not directly aligned to become a part of The Ministry that we are of, then we have Doctrinated ourselves to believe that we have no obligation, or so we think, to be A Witness to that person that is at the point in their life, have reached a Cross Road that The Lord Has Revealed to us as being Spiritual Ambassadors for God, to know exactly what spirit is affecting that individual, to reach out our hands by The Direction of The Holy Ghost to be of Divine Help for such a person that their life that they are currently living is leading them directly to hell.

Now let me explain very carefully so that we may Understand Spiritually: Not everyone will be Saved, that's The Bible; but there are Souls out there that God Requires for us to find through The Leading of The Holy Ghost that is in us. This means that there will be those who signed their lives over to the devil and they know where they are going; those of us who are Spiritually Focused in God will See these persons and the spirits that are influencing their decisions, and the difference will be Manifested within us to know if we are lead to speak to that person, because we would have Identified that God Has Anointed us to Speak to the spirit or spirits within the life of that person, that the Soul will not be Destroyed.

Truth, we cannot touch any or everything that speaks to spirits that affect others, until that time of Release has taken place from God to Give us The Anointing to Overcome those spirits. This is speaking of different Levels in God.

Now that I've made that clear we can move on with the Topic. About three months ago, I went to A Gas Station that I've always purchased gas from; now this Testimony will allow my Readers to

Understand the importance of Being Led by God, and to Allow The Spirit of God to Manifest within our Vessel. I went to A Gas Station, where I regularly buy gas. The person who served me has always been serving me gas; but that morning The Spirit of God within me was confronted with the spirits that were now in full manifestation of the person that was serving me gas for my Vehicle.

Note: The person never said something to me in a manner that would cause offence, neither did the person say anything at all; the person came and I told the person the amount of gas I needed, the person never said anything but went ahead and did the job. It was then while I was being served, I Felt The Presence of God and The Voice of God Followed; and The Lord Said:

"Tell that person that they will Become A True Worshipper for Me".

I Obeyed The Voice of The Lord, I told the person what The Lord Said; I've never had a conversation with this person ever, beside telling that person the amount of gas I needed. After telling the person what The Manifestation of The Voice of God Said, I realized that the person began to look at me different, the person said to me:

"Are You A Pastor"?

I said yes, I am. The person began to open up to me, by letting me know that they grew up in Church and Backslide, and know not how they are going to find their way back; the person gave me all the excuse why they cannot go back into Church, in all this I was **Persistent** because I know what I Felt before I receive The Word from God pertaining to this person's life.

The person then began to Cry and opened up even further for me to understand what the spirits in that person are directing that person to do. The person told me that they had made up their Mind that this life is just too stressful and that they had decided that it was time to commit suicide.

When I heard that I realized that God Is Truly In Love with this person, because if I'm not Led to speak to a person then I will not open my mouth.

When I saw what type of spirits I was now dealing with, I rushed home and printed some Messages that I knew would have broken that Influence of the devil from the life of someone that I knew God Loves; I gave that person my number and I took that person number, I gave that person the assurance to know that I will be Praying every day, three time for the day, I will be Praying and The People of God within The Church will be Praying also.

I called that person every day and visited that person for the first week while that person was reading the Messages that I had given to that person. After a week I realized that there were a lot of Improvements but the spirits was still lingering. I continued to flood this person with Messages and Testimonies and Prayers with Fasting also for this person. After three weeks of continual Prayer with the Prayer group and Fasting for this person, I realized that the spirits of suicide got the Message; and The Message was and still is:

"This Is God's Property, Back Off".

After a month I was encouraging this person to now give their life over to God by telling that person to agree to Baptize in The Name of The Lord Jesus Christ. The person told me that they were in conversation with their mother, and have been convinced that if they are to Serve God again, it must be in the Church that the Mother is attending, which is the same Church that she was attending before. I looked on the person and I said to that person:

Whether you Serve God at the Church you
were going to or decide to Serve God with my

Assembly; Who is The Winner? Is it not God! I told the person that as long as they are directed to now Serve The Living God, then my Job has been fulfilled. God never Told me that you were going to be a part of my Assembly; The Lord Said to Tell this person that they will become A True Worshipper for Him.

I'm Inspired to write this Message today being the 1st of May 2018, because I stopped by the Gas Station this morning and asked the person how are things; the person looked at me in a Bold Confident manner and said things are good Pastor; and I have set my date for Baptism, I am going to Serve The Living God. My response to these words were; To God Be The Glory, Great Things He Has Done.

God Wins Again, one more Soul that was scheduled for destruction has escaped the fire of hell. To God Be The Glory. I let that person know that I will always be praying for their continual Success in God, and the person's response to me was: I Know Pastor, and thank you for your Messages and your Prayers.

I made sure that I made every effort that I do not disclose the person's name or gender because of the delicacy of the Information that is being shared. Therefore, It will be observed that there is certain grammar that is used to best explain the passage of this Testimony.

It must now be understood that God is not only found in one Denomination of A Church, but rather by The Revelations of God, The Lord Allowed me to Understand that there is Levels of His Manifestation in every Church that is calling upon The Name of The Saviour, that is indeed Serving God in Spirit and in Truth. Some Church denominations has A Higher Revelation which brings forth A Higher Anointing of Manifestation than others, but in God's Eye there is still and Only remains to be One Church, with the Manifestation being that of **SPIRIT AND TRUTH.**

Therefore, Let us not be desirous to watch the buildings of The Church or the people that attends that Church, neither let us watch the Names of the Denomination of Churches; let us rather be Focused to Become The Spirit of God and live for God In His Truth, because this is the only Manifestation that Proves that we are in fact The Church, The Bride of Christ that is Ready and Waiting for The Bridegroom Jesus Christ The Saviour of Mankind.

The Lord is Sending out A Call for Lively Stones, and this is The Message:

"Seek to Become of The Attitude of Philip". In Acts Chapter 8:26-40.

This Scripture Reveals that Philip met a man of Ethiopia, of which God's Main Purpose was for Philip to Reveal to the man The Revelations of The Word of God and then to get him Baptized; after this was done The Spirit of God Removed Philip completely from the presence of this man. God Allowed this man to receive enough proof that there is A God and that He Died for the sins of Mankind.

Therefore, So are we Called through The Leading of The Holy Ghost, we must Help those who we can help to break the spiritual control that is currently affecting their lives. That person that you took time out to help will one day be of help to someone else that is in need of earnest help.

Here is a Secret that many have not yet understood; when someone has been delivered from a spirit or spirits that was affecting their life; even though there is no more evidence of the spirits to now control that person's life, the experience of life that has passed still remains with that person, therefore, That person will find himself to be The Best Tool that God Will Use to now Deliver another person in the future that will be affected by that same type of spirit or spirits.

Therefore, When we are Delivered, just remember that we are Delivered that we will be of help to someone in the future through The Leading of God Almighty that they too will be Delivered from that spirit or spirits that is being a Dictator for their Lives.

To God Be All Glory, Honor and Praise, From The Ministry of The Church of Jesus Christ Fellowship, Savannah Cross, Jamaica, West Indies. From The Instrument of God, Pastor Lerone Dinnall, God Bless.

The Attitude Of Being A Son Of God, Just Like Philip.

The Red Eye Monster.

Message # 63   Date Started March 23, 2017
                                 Date Finalized April 1, 2017.

Greeting in The Mighty Name of Jesus Christ, happy to be writing another Inspiring Message for the benefit of myself and my Generation and also for The Family of God. I know that after we have finished reading this Message that God's People will become a lot more Knowledgeable concerning a member of our body that is one of the Entrance to feed our Souls. The saying is true:

"For every Action, there is an equal Reaction".

And the Action of our Eyes to see and then to Lust for those things which we have seen, it then brings forth the Reaction of Sin, of which before we saw there was absolutely no desire or intention of needing anything. Being A Child of God, a person has to become careful because the Devil is out seeking for more and more Souls, and one of his main weapon is to use the desire of the eyes to Lust, thus allowing many who are walking with God to hang up their Salvation just to pick up that which the World has exposed, thus causing God's People to lose their Focus of God and their Inheritance.

I recalled my Grandmother Evangelist Mother Cecilia Whitfield gave her Testimony in Church, regarding her Experience of Travelling. Mother Whitfield Warns The Church that they must be very Careful of when they Travel, because it is found out that the Attractions of this World is very Enticing, that if we has Children of God, if we have not yet found our strength in God, then it is a Fact that when we are exposed to the Glamor and Fashions of this life, it is evident that the opportunity are so attractive that A Child of God may Hang Up their Salvation for any and every opportunity to receive of what the World has to offer through the Lust of our Desire.

The Red Eye Monster is in no wise speaking about someone who we might know, but it is a Fact that this Topic is speaking about the man we see when we look in the mirror; that man, that have not yet become fully Engrafted to what The Word of God Ask us to Become in order to Overcome this World. We can basically do A Study on the Temptation that The Lord Jesus Christ had to endure, in order to Overcome, then we will realize that with every Test, it was based on the first and main desires of that which a man may require at the very time that the Test was being administered; And this is what we have to be careful of. The devil knows the History of Man's Weakness, and he also knows that each one of those weaknesses goes back to the Attraction of The Foundation Seed of Iniquity which brought forth Envy that was initially planted in man the very moment Adam and Eve Disobeyed God.

The Term Red Eye speaks to a person that has fallen for the same Trap that our Forefathers fell for; the desire of becoming better or having more, not realizing that God Has Already Given to us The Very Best of who we are; we then desire something that is not for us, and may never be ours; by not having the knowledge to know that, if God Did Not Command for us to have what was placed in our hands, then the Facts remain, we will lose whatsoever we believe is ours to have by the main Fact that God Did Not Give it to us, but we went ahead and took it for ourselves.

Psalms 127:1.

**"Except The Lord Build the house, they labour
in vain that build it: Except The Lord Keep the city,
the watchman waketh but in vain".**

The more The People of God Are Hungry to achieve of what
the World has to offer, is the more that desire is going to be fueled,
thus causing God's People to forever find ourselves in a position that
we can never be Satisfied; and this Action or Desires will keep us
going around in circles just like The Children of Israel.

For this Topic I will refer my Readers to examine what The
Word of God Has to Say concerning the desires of a man's eye.

Genesis Chapter 3:6.

**"And when the woman SAW that the tree was
good for food, and that it was pleasant to the EYES,
and a tree to be desired to make one wise, she took
of the fruit thereof, and did eat, and gave also unto
her husband with her; and he did eat".**

This Scripture Makes Reference to us that what is wrong may
not necessarily be something or someone that looks or appear to be
bad or evil; but rather what is evil and wrong is that which God
Command His People Not To **TOUCH,** and through Obedience
did not want to find out why it is that we should not Touch, even
though it looks good for Touching and Eating. That which looks
good and pleasing to the eye in many calculations this has not
demonstrated what character the type of Seed Is, but God Knows
every tree and is familiar with every Seed that comes from every tree;
so the next time The Lord Says Do Not Touch, or Taste, or Handle;

it is Recommended that we do what is our job as Servants and Obey, and stop wanting to find out **WHY**.

Genesis Chapter 30:1-4.

"And when Rachel SAW that she bare Jacob no children, Rachel ENVIED her sister; and said unto Jacob, give me children, or else I die. And Jacob anger was kindled against Rachel: and he said, am I in God's stead, who hath withheld from thee the fruit of the womb? And she said, behold my maid Bilhah, go in unto her; and she shall bear upon my knees, that I may also have children by her. And she gave him Bilhah her handmaid to wife: and Jacob went in unto her".

There are many Marriages today that are in Jeopardy because one member or both members of the Circle have not The Quality of Patience to Wait on God's Time and Promise, therefore, We run ahead and make decisions without The Council of The Almighty God, and find ourselves along with our Relationship in deep waters, basically struggling to survive because we have identify that someone; maybe the next door neighbor has something that we desire, and it is found that we are not willing to wait on God's Time to be Perfected. Therefore, We have prematurely found ourselves in positions that seek to choke the life from our Marriage.

Genesis Chapter 39:7-9.

"And it came to pass after these things, that his master's wife cast her EYES upon Joseph, and she said, Lie with me. But he refused, and said unto his master's wife, behold, my master wotteth not what

is with me in the house, and he hath committed all that he hath to my hand; there is none greater in this house than I; neither hath he kept back anything from me but thee, because thou art his wife: how then can I do this great wickedness, and sin against God?"

The **EYES** is the main entrance to cause the Soul to sin, therefore, We have to be very Careful of what we see with the intention of Desiring to **LUST** for that which we have seen. If we yield to the Temptation of that which we Lust for, then any Actions from this Lust will cause God's People to **SIN**.

2 Samuel Chapter 11:2.

"And it came to pass in an eveningtide, that David arose from off his bed, and walked upon the roof of the king's house: and from the roof he SAW a woman washing herself; and the woman was very beautiful to look upon".

There is a saying that goes like this:

"The Devil finds work for idle hands"!

This was the situation that king David found himself in; it was said that at this time of life king David's purpose was to be at Battle, but he instead sent his Captain Joab with soldiers and stayed behind, and the cost was devastating both to himself, his family and to the history of his Kingdom. This Story gives us a reminder that the Choices we decide to take, will ultimately pave the pathway for our Future and the Future of our Children and their Generation to come.

Joshua Chapter 7:20&21.

"And Achan answered Joshua, and said, indeed I have sinned against The Lord God of Israel, and thus and thus have I done: when I SAW among the spoils a goodly Babylonish garment, and two hundred shekels of silver, and a wedge of gold of fifty shekels weight, then I COVETED them, and took them; and, behold, they are hid in the earth in the midst of my tent, and the silver under it".

Can we just imagine, what if Achan never saw the Babylonish garment and the silvers and gold, could that have saved him from not committing sin?_____.

The answer is No; Achan already possessed in him the Seed of Iniquity which brings forth Envy, thus whatever it is that was there, Achan would have Coveted what he saw, thus causing him to commit the act of Disobedience towards God's Command. On this walk with God, we've got to be very careful to know for a surety of what Seed we are of, because the Seed must bring forth a Tree, and the Tree must bear Fruits.

Proverbs Chapter 23:29-35.

"Who hath woe? Who hath sorrow? Who hath contentions? Who hath babbling? Who hath wounds without cause? Who hath REDNESS OF EYES? They that tarry long at the wine; they that go to seek mixed wine. Look not thou upon the wine when it is red, when it giveth his colour in the cup, when it moveth itself aright. At the last it biteth like a serpent, and stingeth like an adder. Thine eyes shall behold strange women, and thine heart

shall utter perverse things. Yea, thou shalt be as he that lieth down in the midst of the sea, or as he that lieth upon the top of a mast. They have stricken me, shalt thou say, and I was not sick; they have beaten me, and I felt it not: when shall I awake? I will seek it yet again".

Here we have a clear layout for a person with the Characteristics of Red Eye.

Proverbs Chapter 24:1&2.

"Be not thou ENVIOUS against evil men, neither DESIRE to be with them. For their heart studieth destruction, and their lips talk of mischief".

There is no value to desire what the Unrighteous Possess, because all that they possess, they will lose, because it was not gained in Righteousness, and Righteousness is the only Foundation.

Proverbs Chapter 27:20.

"Hell and destruction are never full; so the EYES of man are never satisfied".

Ecclesiastes Chapter 1:8.

"All things are full of labour; man cannot utter it: the EYE is not satisfied with seeing, nor the ear filled with hearing".

Let us be careful of what we **SEE** with the desire to **LUST** for that which we have seen; because the more we see, the more we are going to have the desire to continue to see and to Lust for that which we have seen. I have started a new diet in my life, and this is to Block my eyes from anything I think that God Does Not Want me to See.

St Matthew Chapter 5:27-30.

"Ye have heard that it was said by them of old time, thou shalt not commit adultery: But I say unto you, that whosoever LOOKETH on a woman to LUST after her hath committed adultery with her already in his heart. And if thy right eye offend thee, pluck it out, and cast it from thee: for it is profitable for thee that one of thy members should perish, and not that thy whole body should be cast into hell. And if thy right hand offend thee, cut it off, and cast it from thee: for it is profitable for thee that one of thy members should perish, and not that thy whole body should be cast into hell".

In this text, The Lord Is Clearly Demonstrating the Importance of a person being able to enter Heaven at any cost necessary. Now it may sound Barbaric to do what The Lord Command for His People to Do; but we need to remember that this Earth is only our Testing Ground, a life of Free Will, to identify how Obedient we are to God's Command, to thus find ourselves being Qualified to walk through The Gates of Heaven, thus Achieving that which has **NO END**.

Eyes cannot compare to what we will receive; Hands, Feet, Mouth, Education, Opportunities, Jobs, Money, Husbands and Wives, Children, not even this life cannot compare. Whatever we have to do to make it in, **DO IT!** The word cut off and plucked out in the scripture can also illustrate that we need to stop the functions and operations of that which will lead us to destruction, no matter how close that member is to us.

Here is an easy Demonstration to pluck out an eye, if that eye has become offensive to The Spirit man or to God's Commandments:

> **Start to Train that very eye to no longer have the desire to see that which caused the offence of lust; and by doing this, Spiritually you have plucked out that eye, thus allowing yourself now to see what God Needs for you to See.**

> **St Matthew Chapter 6:22&23.**

> **"The light of the body is the eye: if therefore thine eye be single, thy whole body shall be full of light. But if thine eye be evil, thy whole body shall be full of darkness. If therefore the light that is in thee be darkness, how great is that darkness!"**

I remember reading this Scripture when I was younger, and I never understood what it meant, therefore I went to Bishop Austin Whitfield, and this is what he Said:

> **"Titus Chapter 1:15. Unto the pure all things are pure: but unto them that are defiled and unbelieving is nothing pure; but even their mind and conscience is defiled. He also said that the word Single in the Text, demonstrates the word Holiness; therefore, If a person is living In The**

Will and Commands of God, that person's life will be filled with The Light of God".

St John Chapter 9:1-3.

"And Jesus Passed by, He Saw a man which was blind from his birth. And His Disciples asked Him, saying, Master, who did sin, this man, or his parents, that he was born blind? Jesus Answered, neither hath this man sinned, nor his parents: but that The Works of God Should Be Made Manifest in him".

What Eyes cannot see, Heart will never desire to have, therefore Lust is Killed. The only sin this person could now commit would be the sin of Blasphemy.

1 John Chapter 2:16.

"For all that is in the world, the lust of the flesh, and the lust of the EYES, and the pride of life, is not of The Father, but is of the world".

This Text is speaking of a Level that not many Christians have come to the understanding to receive; and the sooner we reach that Level, the easier the walk with Christ will become.

Note: If a person will become Discipline enough to Conquer The Red Eye Monster; then you're looking at the same person that will be able to Conquer life's pathway of Free Will, thus there is nothing that can stop that person from being Prepared to Inherit The Kingdom of God; Facts.

All Glory, Honor and Praise Forever Be unto The Only One God, Jesus Christ The Lamb of God. I remain the Humble Servant of The Only Living God. May God Continue to Bless, Keep, Sanctify to Make Holy His People for His Coming. From The Ministry of The Church of Jesus Christ Fellowship, Savannah Cross, Jamaica, West Indies. God Bless. Pastor Lerone Dinnall.

Be Alert of The Red Eye Monster.

What Will You Do When Your Friends Become Your Enemy?

Message # 42   Date Started April 16, 2017

Date Finalized April 23, 2017.

Exodus Chapter 33:11.

"And The Lord Spake unto Moses face to face, as a man speaketh unto his friend. And he turned again into the camp: but his servant Joshua, the son of Nun, a young man, departed not out of the Tabernacle".

2 Chronicles Chapter 20:7.

"Art not thou our God, who didst drive out the inhabitants of this land before thy people Israel, and gavest it to the seed of Abraham thy friend forever?"

Proverbs Chapter 17:17.

"A friend loveth at all times, and a brother is born for adversity".

Proverbs Chapter 18:24.

"A man that hath friends must shew himself friendly: And there is a friend that sticketh closer than a brother".

St John Chapter 15:12-17.

"This is My commandment, that ye love one another, as I Have Loved you. Greater love hath no man than this, that a man lay down his life for his friends. Ye are My friends, if ye do whatsoever I Command you. Henceforth I Call you not servants; for the servant knoweth not what his lord doeth: but I Have Called you friends; for all things that I Have Heard of My Father I Have Made Known unto you. Ye have not chosen Me, but I Have Chosen you, and Ordained you, that ye should go and bring forth fruit, and that your fruit should remain: that whatsoever ye shall ask of The Father in My Name, He May Give It you. These things I Command you, that ye Love One another".

I Give Praise, Honor, and Glory, Alleluia to The Omnipotent God, The Omnipresent God, The Omniscient God, The Saviour of Mankind, Jesus Christ The Spotless Lamb of God. It's truly a Privilege to be using the Talent of writing as a Ministry for all God's People and especially for those who have not yet accepted the Invitation to accept Jesus Christ as their personal and only Saviour.

My hope and desire is for all those who would have come in contact with this Message to witness The Anointing of Truth, that our eyes will no more be blocked by the covering of this World's Teaching; but by The Anointing of The Almighty God we will be Loosed to discover that there can only be One True Living Friend that will never turn His Back, nor will He Forget us when we have passed the best of what we are ordained to become. The God that Remains Faithful, throughout all Times and Seasons, and Forget not our Sacrifice; But Will Always Remember that which we have done for God, even when we have passed from this life to the next; and even then our Sacrifice still lives on in His Thoughts towards our Generation that should come after us. A Friend in which there is no Diluting, but Remains Strong to show forth Kindness and Favors to His Inheritance Forever and Ever, Amen.

Let us have a look at what the Dictionary has to explain about the word Friend. According to the Oxford Dictionary It States:

> **"A person that one likes and knows well; a person who supports a particular cause or organization".**

The Webster Dictionary States:

> **"A person attached to another by feelings of affection or personal regard. A person who gives assistance; patron; supporter. A person who is on good terms with another; a person who is not hostile".**

The Illustrated Bible Dictionary States:

> **"A person whom one loves and trusts; close companion or Comrade".**

The Holman Illustrated Bible Dictionary States:

"Close trusting relationship between two people; loving companionship".

This Dictionary also states that what best describes a relationship of Friendship outside of God's Relationship with Abraham and for those who Obey Him, would be the Relationship that David and Jonathan portrayed in the Book of 1 Samuel Chapter 18:1-4. Which Says:

> **"And it came to pass, when he had made an end of speaking unto Saul, that the soul of Jonathan was knit with the soul of David, and Jonathan loved him as his own soul. And Saul took him that day, and would let him go no more home to his father's house. Then Jonathan and David made a covenant, because he loved him as his own soul. And Jonathan stripped himself of the robe that was upon him, and gave it to David, and his garments, even to his sword, and to his bow, and to his girdle".**

Now if we could observe carefully, both Dictionaries being Oxford and Webster, these could only explain that which the Physical Man could identify what a friend is or should be. On the other hand, both Illustrated Bible Dictionaries gave a more in depth meaning of what the meaning of a friend is composed of; obviously through the demonstrations and examples of what took place in Bible History.

The Lord Revealed to me that becoming A Friend of God Requires A Continual Spirit of Obedience to which God Has Predestinated who it is that will be able to reach A Qualified State of obtaining this precious Favor. The Lord Revealed that no man by his own ability can work for such a Title as this, but rather it is God that

Foresees and have Chosen from The Foundation of the Earth who it is that will become entitled to wear such a Favor as this.

The Lord Also Revealed that it is God that Gives to that person The Appetite to Receive of The Spirit of Obedience, that, that person will be able to make all the right decisions on life's road of Free Will.

The Lord Revealed that everything in this life and in the life to come is already **FIXED** before The Foundation of the World. There is no Surprise, there are no Mistakes, there are no Confusions. Those who are to be Saved, must be Saved; those who are to Elevate from being A Servant to A Friend of God are already Chosen for that Task and Destiny, and no one can take that Anointing away from them; those who are to become Pastors, Teachers, Preachers, Overseers, Elders, Bishops Is Fixed; and it is also Predestined for those who will be a part of Church for the purpose of only warming the bench. Those who are going to Hell are already on the pathway to Hell; it doesn't matter how many time we Preach and Teach and Testify, it won't change them, because they are already on a path towards Destruction; The Word of God Can Only Bring Forth Change to those who have prepared **THE GOOD GROUND.**

The Lord Revealed that Teaching and Preaching, Testimony must continue, even to those who are not Chosen, to bring proof to The Word of God that those who heard The Words of Life Cannot Accept It, because the Seed of Iniquity which births Envy still remains in them.

The Lord Revealed that the Wheat and Tares have to grow together, as it is those who are not fully persuaded must remain to sharpen the lives of those who are fully persuaded. Therefore, We will never get rid of False Brethren from The Church, and there will always be someone that will be doing the opposite of what The Word of God Ask us to Fulfill, just to allow The Fear of God to Remain on The Righteous Seed. St Matthew Chapter 7:13-14 Says:

"Enter ye in at the strait gate: and broad is the way, that leadeth to destruction, and many there be which go in thereat: because strait is the gate, and narrow is the way, which leadeth unto life, and few there be that find it".

And again The Lord Revealed that Becoming A Friend of God Is A Title and Favor that remains in The Seed and Lineage of that person, meaning, even when our time on Earth has ended, that Mantle of Favors continues for the Generation of that person's Lineage, and nothing can stop The Anointing that Exist. It can be the comparison to that of God Making Mountains on Earth to always be above the Valleys of the Earth, the Seas, Rivers and Plain; just because the Primary / Foundation Servant chose to Obey The Direction and The Operation of The Spirit of God.

The Question is asked by this Topic, which Says: What will you do when your Friends become your Enemy?_____.

There are always two pathways to this life that we live, which therefore Manifest the Operation of two different works of the spirit. And while it is that there be many that can Testify to the Fact that they have encountered the Manifestation of True Friends; that Manifestation is Governed by The Operation and The Movement of The Spirit that Moves in that person; and if it be that, that person have lost the pathway on which they had travel on to Entertain that type of Spirit being A Friend of God, then it is at that time that this person would have found themselves on the other path to entertain a spirit of Iniquity which births Envy which is of the Devil, of which its movement is in complete contradiction to what the previous Spirit of Love was doing and was Manifesting; and all these events takes place in the same body; and if this person is not Discipline to take hold and to Maintain The Commandments of God, to make sure that he or she walks in God's Precepts, this person will never remain A Friend to others.

In a NutShell, The Lord Is Demonstrating to us that unless those who we call Friends remain under The Guidance and Influence of The Word of God, then time will Reveal that such a person can never and will never be of the capability to remain being A Friend. By The Revelation of The Word of God, those who are to be Friends to The Children of God are already those who are Born of The Kingdom of God's Glory.

There are many things We The Children of God stretch our limits in, and one of those things is to see how best we can entertain those who are not of The Kingdom of God, to try by our influence to see if we can actually keep those friends which were a part of our lives when we were not Saved, to see if the possibility exist that darkness can be mixed with light of which it can't. And to this state of Mind of believing that this event can actually exist; it may take us years to be Born in the belief that there is just no mixing between Light and Darkness.

Light is Attracted to Light and A Higher Glory of Light, while Darkness is Attracted to Darkness, and seeketh not to become of The Characteristics of Light; therefore, Children of God have got to understand that the only way a person can be Changed from Darkness to Light, will not take an Action of remaining to be a So Called Friend, but instead it Requires Action only by The Blood of Jesus Christ to Wash Away that person's Darkness / Sin, to Enable them to Become A Child of The Light. And only when that person has been Born to become Light, can that person actually know what it is like to be A Friend of God; and if they are now A Friend of God, then it is evident that they will be and remain to be A Friend to The Family of God.

Note: A Friend is not a Friend because of one good action or because they say so, but rather a Friend is a Friend that remains being a Friend through every life's challenge; and will never change their opinion of you because your back is turned or you have become ill, or even when this life has come to an end and there is nothing more that we can do under the Sun. A Friend is now A Friend because He Remembers our Sacrifice, and Shows Kindness to our Generation. And who is that Friend?_____.

No one else but our Lord and Saviour Jesus Christ, and those who are Children of The Birth, Blood and Testimony of Jesus Christ.

There is A Message in The Scriptures that Jesus Christ Demonstrated to allow us to Understand who it Is that is to be considered as His Family and also Our family.

St Matthew Chapter 12:46-50.

"While He yet Talked to the people, behold, His mother and His brethren stood without, desiring to speak with Him. Then one said unto Him, behold, Thy mother and Thy brethren stand without, desiring to speak with Thee. But He Answered and said unto him that told Him, Who is My mother? And who are My brethren? And He Stretched Forth His Hand towards His Disciples, and Said, behold My mother and My brethren! For whosoever shall do The Will of My Father which is in Heaven, the same is My brother, and sister, and mother".

So is it that The Children of God have got to be Wise to Understand to be Knowledgeable, to thus identify who it is that we can actually say are our Friends; because, If it is that our Friends is not Identified In The Will of God, then we are only looking at another person who is destined to fail us. And it's not like they planned to be a Failure; it's just that they do not have the Ingredients of The Seed of Life in them to be of The Likeness of that Eternal Friend, therefore, they automatically found themselves on a pathway that they are already Failures.

There is a song that Reveals A Message in the words by Saying:

"Only your friends Know your Secret". By: Bob Marley.

There is A Lesson to be learnt from this song in regards to this Message that is being read; and The Message Is Clear:

Be careful of those who you esteem as your friends, because if it is found that this friend is not on The Foundation of The Word of God, then it is A Fact, this Friend would have already failed you, even if it has not happened as yet.

And take A Wild Guess of what will happen when your Friends do Fail you:

That's it!

That Friend or Friends knows your secret. Now, Looking back to what The Topic Says: What will you do when your Friends become your Enemy?_____.

What will you do?_____.

There is however A Friend that I Can Invite every person to, and His Name Is Jesus Christ, The Saviour of All Mankind; there is nothing that you can tell this Friend and wonder if He's Going to Change, or wonder if your secrets will be Revealed; He Is The Friend That Will Stick Closer than A Brother, He Will Not Leave you nor Will He Ever Forsake you, He's Always There, Always on time and Never Late, even when it seems like He is Late or is not going to Show Up; A Friend that Fills all Conditions, and Will Continue to be A Friend to our Children even when we are gone; Ever Faithful, Ever Loving and Ever Caring God.

Unto The Most Excellent Father Be All Glory, Honor and Praise from Beginning to Eternity. From The Ministry of The Church of Jesus Christ Fellowship, Savannah Cross, Jamaica, West Indies. From your Faithful Servant, your Brother and Minister, Pastor Lerone Dinnall. God Bless.

What Will You Do When Your Friends Become Your Enemy?

What Hands Don't Work, Let Not Heart Desire To Have, WARNING!

Message # 52

Date Started August 17, 2017.
Date Finalized August 17, 2017.

Genesis Chapter 3:17-19.

"And to Adam He Said, because thou hast hearkened unto the voice of thy wife, and hast eaten of the tree, of which I Commanded thee, Saying, Thou Shalt Not Eat of it: Cursed is the ground for thy sake; in sorrow shalt thou eat of it all the days of thy life; Thorns and thistles shall it bring forth to thee; and thou shalt eat the herb of the field; In the sweat of thy face shalt thou eat bread, till thou return unto the ground; for out of it was thou taken: for dust thou art, and unto dust shalt thou return".

Greetings in The Mighty Name of Jesus Christ The Soon Coming King, The Savior of Mankind. It is a Privilege for me that I am placed in this Position to write Inspiring Messages. There are some lessons in life that a person has to experience for themselves; meaning that no matter how often someone tries to warn us concerning the Impending Danger that is ahead or that exists, we would most of the time want to experience for ourselves if this is truly the way it really is.

This desire of wanting to find out for ourselves is A Disease in our **DNA**, that same Seed of **INIQUITY** which births **ENVY**, that stems from the Foundation life of Adam and Eve; which sees God Giving Clear Instructions to Adam and Eve pertaining to what will destroy their Souls, Exiting their Spiritual life from the Upright position with God, and not only their Souls but also all the Souls that would have spring from their Generation representing the Entire Human-race.

It is Amazing to see how Destructive the eyes of a man can truly be, meaning that if this man have not exercise himself to have the Discipline to Train the eyes not to have the desire to want everything that, that eyes have seen; then it would be realized that such a person with the disease of The Red Eye Monster, will only manifest the Desire and Zeal of wanting to obtain everything their eyes have seen, even without the evidence that such a person actually have the necessary funding to purchase that which they desire to have.

I recently heard my Wife in one of her lessons to The Church explaining how it is that we as Christians have to Evolve to a Level that when someone is showing us what they have achieved, to make sure that we put blinders on our eyes, because she came to the discovery that if this is not done; it would lead to us as Christians desiring also that same thing that we have seen someone with; and not knowing that such a person maybe putting on a show because we can never truly know what a person have done to acquire that which they possess.

Because the truth and the Fact of live is that, there are many persons that have signed the deal of an **EASY LIFE** to live, with the requirement being that they have signed over their Souls to the Devil, therefore whatever they would desire to have in this life without the evidence of work being done is easily achieved, but all this comes with a Price. And most of the time the price is to sell our Souls to the Devil, and not only our Souls are at risk, but the contract is also for the Souls of our Generation to come; as such was the case of Adam and Eve.

Because Adam and Eve thought that they have Sinned only for themselves, they were soon to find out that the Sin and the Agreement which they have signed to fulfilled by just Disobeying The Commands of God, this had the Sure Consequences in the Fine Prints of the Agreement that their Generation would also be Trapped under the same Agreement for all times, even though the Children knew nothing of such Agreement; therefore, It is always important for Children of God to make sure that we read to understand the **fineprints.**

Having also learnt my valuable Lesson from my experience with the Bank, I can truly be a Testimony to the Generation to come, especially my personal Generation; to know that they need not to try and find out for themselves, I am in the position to be their Father and Provider on Earth, therefore, Whatever Instructions I've laid out for them is to be compared to Precious Gold.

This is My Testimony: For all my life I have been of the Attitude that Hard Work will bring forth great success, therefore, I positioned myself to work very hard. In the process of reaching the age of thirty, I managed to build my own home, have my own car, and obtain my own Business and also to get Married. I felt good, knowing that I've worked hard and achieved great success. Now the time came that there presented itself a great opportunity for myself and my wife, but the only problem was, in order to receive this opportunity I had to show evidence of some amount of money in my Account to stand has evidence that I can fulfill the payments of such opportunity; being now consumed with the effects of The Red Eye Monster, and seeing other couple seizing the same opportunity to better their lives, I went and did that which I promised myself that I would not have done; I went to the Bank and obtained a Loan, and used my House that I have Built as security for that Loan, with my only problem and responsibility at that time was the Mortgage, Light Bill and Water Bill.

I got the loan from the Bank, Me and my Wife processed all requirements through the Legal Channel to obtain the opportunity. The Summary of what took place after was to be compared to complete disappointment, everything that could go bad, it went bad, and very bad, with the only joy in this experience being the Birth of our first child. And if that wasn't Bad enough, after two years of making payments to the Bank for the Loan we had received, the Bank Transformed to be The Devil himself with all the Demons of Hell accompanying him.

After being able to make Payment for over two (2) years, and finding it now to be a little difficult to maintain payments; the sweet smiling faces of the representatives from the Bank that I first met and was willing to meet with me at any given opportunity to ensure that I have accepted their loan offer; now those same representative grew Vampire's Teeth with the sole purpose being to suck me dry. After two years doing my own calculations, I saw that I would have paid over half of the loan that I had borrowed, only to hear from the Blood Suckers that I have only paid the Interest, and the loan has not yet started to be paid.

It came to a point in my life that everyday and every other day there would be someone calling me from the Bank Saying:

"O Mr. Dinnall, try and make payment of X amount today, or else your house will be put up for sale".

This continued for a while, I sacrificed food in my house to make payments, I sacrificed paying other bills to make payments to these Blood Suckers, I borrowed money from Family and Clients to feed the Bank. The more I paid, the more calls came. I got so frustrated that I wasn't eating the way I should be eating, life now became a Big Stress; seeing that I was in a position that the only thing I needed to pay was the Mortgage, Light and Water bill, and now have move to a place that the Devil and his Demons are sucking me for every ounce of blood that I have, and also knowing that if I never desired other opportunity, I would not have found myself in this position.

This harassment continued until I Look to The Hills from whence cometh my Help; I said Lord Help, because I feel like I'm at the point of dying. The Lord Said:

"Just Let Go, Just Let Go and I Will Do the rest".

I never actually let go until about two months after, when the Bank called me to do their continual Harassment, in that Moment I Remembered The Words of The Lord that Says:

"Just Let Go, and I Will Do the Rest".

I felt The Anointing of God Rushing in my veins, and I said to the Bank Manager go ahead and sell the House because I have no more payments to make to save this House; I also said to the Bank Manager a word which I knew was not my words, I said, when you have sold my house and leave me without a house, what else can you do, can you now take my life away from me? The Bank Manager called two other days, and also another Manager, and the Response was the same:

Sell The House, Take Your Payments And Leave Me Alone.

I also made them a promise because they were determined to sell my house without giving me the option to have a longer period of payment. I told them that they need not to worry about me, because I have learnt my lesson, I have gone through University and back from the experience of the Bank and the lesson is learnt, and I will also make sure that I teach My Wife and My Children these lessons and all those who will hear my words, and the Lesson is this: The Bank is The Gateway to Hell that a person will sell their Souls to the Devil, the workers at the Bank are the Influenced Demons, the workers of that hell, of which anyone that falls in their trap, without The Help of The Almighty God will be destined for Destruction and Hell. I told the Bank Manager, from now on for my life, What hands don't work, My Heart will Never desire to have, and that goes for my Wife and all my Children forever.

After making those statements through The Anointing of The Most High God, it has been eight months now, I haven't heard back from the Bank Managers nor his workers. I continue to seek to try and sell the House while making the payments that I can afford. I know not what the Future holds but I know who has the Future In His Hands, and He Told me to Just Let Go, and He Will Do the rest.

The Lord Allowed me to realize that He Has All Power, and every type and medium of powers has to go through Him. And if God Does Not Sign With His Pen for something to happen, then all those who desire for it to happen, will only be establishing for themselves their own Iniquity which shall be Poured out upon their own heads. Because The Lord Has Revealed that if Judgment is to be established on anyone of His Children; because He Has Already Paid The Price for our Sins. That same Judgment must start from the head of which The Lord Will Establish. The Lord through Comforting Words Said to me:

**"Those who have the power of the pen to write
what should take place in the life of A Child of God,
should also consider that The Father of those who**

141

Trust In Him Has The Divine Pen that He Is Also Prepared to Use"...

The Lord Also Said:

"The True Children of God need not to worry because whatever takes place in this life whether it be destruction or establishment, there will be one thing that will remain and that one thing is the Foundation of The Word of God which is a Fact, are those who Represent The Righteous Seed"...

Therefore, The World can continue to plan all the destruction for The Children of God, the end result will established that the World has fallen in the same Pit they have Dig, because it is The Word of God that Says:

"The Righteous Shall Inherit the Earth"...

To all My Readers, learn from My Mistake, that which the Bank has Acquired, we know not by what means and channel they have acquired such wealth; but one thing I know from My Experience with the Bank, that which they have acquired to offer has a loan to their Customer comes at so high a price that they have to become the full Manifestation of the Devil in order to maintain their Lucrative lifestyle.

Who knows what else they are doing and what they are a part of, what type of system they have joined to establish whatever they have agreed to fulfill; with whatever type of Blood Sacrifice that is necessary for their Business to strive. Come to think about it, what do we truly know about the Banks?

There is a Test I would want my Readers to analyze for themselves, that being to work hard and earn your own money by the sweat of your Face, then you will realize that, that money that you have earned by Sweating carries Weights and Values, but on the other hand, I personally have discovered that the money that the Bank has given for a loan, I don't know if it's Blood Money, but there is a clear difference, that money can never be used to establish a meaningful purpose in your business or for your life, trust me, I'm a hard worker and I have proven it for myself.

The money of a Bank comes with the Disease of being an **Accursed Thing**, that which God Has Asked us in The Book of Joshua Chapter 6:18. To make sure that we Stay Away From and Do Not Touch The Accursed Thing.

> **"And ye, in any wise keep yourself from The Accursed Thing, lest ye make yourself Accursed, when ye take of The Accursed Thing, and make the camp of Israel A Curse, and trouble it".**

We have read what took place with Achan, he took of the Accursed Thing and this brought forth the manifestation that not one of The Children of Israel had the courage any more to stand up and face their enemies because of that which was an Accursed Thing. This is what the money from the Bank reminds me of, an Absent from God's Favor, because of something which is A Curse being in our surroundings. Therefore, No matter how we would seek to try to Spin, Twist, Invest, Build with this money; this money remains in a category that it is just one of the Accursed Things that God Needs us to stay away from. Another word for the Bank Money is called The Dead Money, No Life in it.

In life it is the custom that in order for most people to learn, it is Revealed that they would have to feel for themselves. I hope this will not be the case for those who have read this Message. I

Pray that my Readers would have read and seek to understand for themselves the Risk; and also in everything and in every decision making to make sure that you Consult The Voice of God to ensure that whatever decision that you're going to make, that The Anointing of God's Hand Will Be Able To See you through.

I hope this Message along with My Testimony would have helped My Readers to make sure that you are sure, and to make certain that whatever you're doing financially is in The Will of God The Father. Because by knowing that God Is In It, you will be able to save yourself a lifetime of Mistakes and Misery for both you, your family and your Generation.

I Will Bless The Lord At All Times, May His Praises Continue To Be In My Mouth. To The Only High God, Jesus Christ, The Lamb of God. From The Ministry of The Church of Jesus Christ Fellowship, Savannah Cross, Jamaica, West Indies. From your Friend, Brother and Pastor Lerone Dinnall. God Bless.

- **Watch The fineprints.**
- **Read The fineprints.**
- **Understand The fineprints.**
- **Make Certain That The fineprints Are Legal.**
- **Pray And Fast Concerning The fineprints.**
- **Don't Sign Unless You Have Identified Your Way Through The fineprints With The Help Of God.**
- **Make Certain To Keep A Copy Of The fineprints.**

What Hands Don't Work, Let Not Heart Desire To Have. It's A Warning Not An Opinion!

Waiting On God's Time...

Message # 85   Date Started October 8, 2017
Date Finalized October 8, 2017.

Galatians Chapter 4:1-7.

"Now I say, that the heir, as long as he is a child, differeth nothing from a servant, though he be lord of all; But is under tutors and governors until the time appointed of the father. Even so we, when we were children, were in bondage under the elements of the world: But when the fullness of the time was come, God Sent Forth His Son, made of a woman, made under the law, To redeem them that were under the law, that we might receive the adoption of sons. And because ye are sons, God Hath Sent Forth The Spirit of His Son into your hearts, Crying, Abba, Father. Wherefore thou art no more a servant, but a son; and if a son, then an heir of God through Christ".

I Will Bless The Lord At All Times, May His Praises Continue To Be In My Mouth. Happy and Privileged am I to be writing another Message Inspired by The Heavenly Father, Jesus Christ The Only Lamb Of God.

Waiting on God's Time; The Scripture Reveals that for many of us who are to be Born of God to Become Sons of God, we are Delayed from The Divine Destined Purpose for the simple fact, that being, that we are still children in need of Training to become what God Would Have for us to Become. A Son of God Is A Mature Upstanding Child of God, which has been Given The Intelligence of The Mind of God; thus the Attitude of A Child to make mistakes are no longer found in The Characteristics of A Son of God.

There are times in this life that we are found fallen in the spirit of Frustration and Depression, reason being; we know what God Says He's Going to Do, and we believe in all that God Says He's Going to Do, but for some reason we are fallen short of the comfort of the heart to understand that man's time will never be God's Time. Therefore, This Topic is being written to help those of us to be born in the Attitude to understand that we must seek to wait on God's Time. Man can never bring forth the Promises that are Wrapped Up In God's Time; therefore, There is nothing that a man can promise you that will Force God's Hand to Bring forth Destiny.

Father Abraham is a prime example of God's Time. After Receiving and Believing God's Word for A Blessing that would see his generation becoming The Blessing of The Lord; Abraham through time made a few mistakes, because he was not completely reliant on what God Had Said, believing for some reason that he needed to help God on His Quest to make his life A Blessing.

I remember sharing a word with The Saints, and it goes like this:

When God Speak A Word, if He Knew He Was Not Going To Fulfill What He Has Spoken, then He Would Not Have Said It; therefore, If God Speaks A Word Of Promise In Our Lives, then, He Has Already Established that which He Spake In His Time.

It took Abraham twenty-five years to Receive the foundation of that same Blessing. There is something that I've observed concerning God's Blessing, and I've shared this with a lot of Saints. Whenever it is that God Makes A Promise, there is always little or no details Given to that person of how such A Promise is going to be Fulfilled. I've found out that the consciousness of our Minds are so limited that for God to Bring us into The Revelation step by step what He's Going To Allow To Be Fulfilled in our lives, if this is Revealed with also the period of time that it will take to manifest; I tell you the truth, for all of us, we could not even receive the Volume of Information, and even if it were possible that we could receive the Information; upon realizing what is Required by us as A Sacrifice to fulfill The Requirements, we would not even move to walk in that Purpose.

We've found out that while Moses was being Led By God, he knew that God Was Leading him, but through what channel God Was Leading him was A Complete Mystery. After being Triumphant in taking God's People out of Egypt by The Leading of God's Mighty Hand; Moses Knew The Destination, which is the land of Canaan, but it was only when he got to The Red Sea which was in front of him, Pharaoh's army behind him and mountains on both sides; it was only at that time when the people cried to Moses and Moses Cried to God, that God Brought Forth The Revelation to Moses that he must use what he have in his hand to allow The Red Sea to become a Dry ground for The Children of Israel to pass over.

Could you just imagine when God Called Moses at The Burning Bush, this same Moses that was fearful for his life, that never saw himself even being able to speak to Pharaoh much less to be in the same presence that Pharaoh was in; Could you just imagine God Laying Out The Dictionary at Moses feet in that Burning Bush! Could Moses at that time be able to manage The Volume of Information and Requirements that were needed by him to fulfill for God's Purpose?_____. I think not.

So is it with us that are Serving God; we are given The Promise of our Divine Destined Purpose and Blessing; but we know not how, when, by what means, or by what way, we do not know The Time or The Seasons that The Lord Have Cemented In His Own Will. But this we know, God's Promises Are Fixed To Bring Forth God's Pleasure / Glory, not man. Therefore, A Child of God waiting on God's Time has to exercise The Spirit of Patience, because man's time has to be buried in order for God's Time to spring forth. It's wrapped up in these words:

"My Glory Will I Not Give To Another"...

There is no way when God Works, can man lift his hands and say I have done this. But when God Has Manifested, man will fall to his knees and Declare:

"To God Be The Glory Great Things He Has Done"...

I Hope that this Message Was and Is A Blessing to whosoever gets a chance to read it. To God Be The Glory Great Things He Has Done. From The Ministry of The Church of Jesus Christ Fellowship, Savannah Cross, Jamaica, West Indies. Pastor Lerone Dinnall. God Bless.

Waiting On God's Time Carries Less Pain, TRUTH!

The Other gods...

Message # 113   Date Started March 10, 2019
Date Finalized March 10, 2019.

Deuteronomy Chapter 6:4.

"Hear, O Israel: The Lord our God Is One Lord"!

Hear All Nations, Languages, Cultures and Dominions, The Lord God Almighty Is One God!

I Give Honor and Praise to The Only God Who is One and Remaineth to Be One to all People, Nations, Cultures and Dominions from Beginning to Eternity, Whose Manifestation is seen through The Vessel of Jesus Christ. Privileged am I to be found in this Position that I am found worthy through The Blood of Jesus Christ to be A Vessel that God Can Use.

The spirit of Ignorance is a Sin, it however carries a lesser punishment than that of a person who is well knowledgeable of what they are doing. There are many times even myself read the Scriptures which profess that we should have no other gods in relationship with The True and Living God, and that's where it stops, in the Attitude of just reading a Scripture Which tells us what not to do. But here is the Big Question:

What and Who Are The Other gods?_____.

Have we ever taken it upon ourselves to do a research of what
The Bible was Demonstrating as the other gods?

_____.

The Relationship with God must be compared to that of A
Spiritual Ladder that each Believer must find themselves to now seek
to climb, in order for us to reach the Coveted Anointing of being in
Relationship with The Eternal Spirit of God that sees every Release
from God that spells Revelation, such a Child of God will be first in
line to receive of The Divine Approval of God's Speech.

It must be the understanding in the lives of God's People that
Relationship with God can be compromised with the effects of what
The Lord was Commanding The Children of Israel to make certain
that within their personal Relationship with God it must never be
Mixed with the manifestations of the other gods.

Therefore, The Question is still being Asked, What and Who
are the other gods?_____.

The simplest Answer that I can give to God's People is to
identify within your own Relationship with God of that which cause
you the individual to stay Connected with The God of The Universe,
then it must become the understanding born in us to also identify
that the other gods is any and every person that is not serving The
True and Living God The way you the individual have now come
to identify that this is The Way that a person must Attract God to
Remain in Relationship with The God of The Universe.

St Matthew Chapter 22:34-40.

**"But when the Pharisees had heard that
He had put the Sadducees to silence, they were
gathered together. Then one of them, which was a
lawyer, asked Him a question, tempting Him, and
saying, Master, which is the great commandment
in the law? Jesus Said unto him, Thou shalt love**

The Lord thy God with all thy heart, and with all thy Soul, and with all thy Mind. This is the first and great commandment. And the second is like unto it, Thou shalt love thy neighbour as thyself. On these two commandments hang all the law and the Prophets".

A Child of God that is seeking to remain in Relationship with The Father has to exercise these two Disciples to a Touch, Love God with Heart, Soul and Mind, The Three Active Responses of Mankind Relationship with God. And the next is to Love our Neighbour as ourselves.

Now here is another Question that will help in the discussion of this Topic: Who is Our Neighbour?_____.

Our Neighbour is the direct Replica of The Manifestation of God, therefore, each time we have a look on our Neighbour, we will identify at all times the ingredients of Spiritual Growth; we might not be at the same level of that which our neighbour is at, or they might not be at the same level of that which we are at, but there is a Spiritual Reflection that Manifest within our Heart, Soul and Mind, The Three Active Responses of Mankind that this person wears the same Standards of that which yourself seeks to Manifest for The Glory of God.

Note: Your Neighbour will always Sharpen your Spiritual life to Climb The Spiritual Ladder of God's Relationship. Therefore manifesting in an Individual's life the Activity of Iron Sharpening Iron. Because once we are forced to grow by those who are in our Circle, then our lives will automatically force others to grow that are directly a part of our circle which represents our Neighbour. This does not means that those who are our Neighbours will never make a mistake that causes that person to sin, but it will be identified that our Neighbours will bear the same Reflection of that which we would have done when we have sinned before God to ensure that we confess our sins before God, wash our Garments and seek to continue the climb of Spiritual Growth. The Neighbours that are Manifested for our lives will never seek to remain in sin, because remaining in sin will always kill the Spiritual Growth of that person who seeks to climb The Spiritual Ladder of God's Relationship.

God Never Designed for us to travel this pathway by ourselves, but rather, this Journey is Fixed with the Puzzle of The Map for our lives to Find, to Identify and to Remain in Relationship with those who are A Spiritual Neighbour for our walk with Christ.

Not everyone that is attending Church like yourself is your neighbour, we might be on the Choir for the Church, and yes this is a Family coming together to fulfill the mission of worship for God, but the fact still remains that after Worship has ended for God, it will be identified by yourself that it's not everyone on the Choir The Spirit of God Grants Permission to be directly linked to your life that will resemble that being A Neighbour. And that's a Fact!

The other gods which manifest the activities of other people, if they are now allowed by us to pattern their spirits to our environment, then this will bring forth a crack in our Vessels for God's Will Being Done within our lives, therefore resulting in a leakage within our own Spiritual lives, that when God Pours The Anointing within us to Manifest His Glory, because of The Crack established by people which represents other gods, we will not be able to demonstrate and to Manifest for God the way God Would Desire for us to Manifest for His Glory.

Deuteronomy Chapter 6:12-16.

"Then beware lest thou forget The Lord, which brought thee forth out of the land of Egypt, from the house of bondage. Thou shalt fear The Lord thy God, and Serve Him, and shalt swear by His Name. <u>Ye shall not go after other gods, of the</u>

gods of the people which are round about you; (For The Lord thy God Is A Jealous God among you) lest The Anger of The Lord thy God Be Kindled against thee, and Destroy thee from off the face of the Earth. Ye shall not tempt The Lord your God, as ye tempted Him in Massah".

Joshua Chapter 7:10-12.

"And The Lord Said unto Joshua, Get thee up; wherefore liest thou thus upon thy face? Israel hath sinned, and they have also transgressed My Covenant which I Commanded them: for they have even taken of the accursed thing, and have also stolen, and dissembled also, and they have put it even among their own stuff. Therefore the children of Israel could not stand before their enemies, because they were accursed: neither will I be With you anymore, Except ye destroy the accursed from among you".

Deuteronomy Chapter 7:25&26.

"The graven images of their gods shall ye burn with fire: thou shalt not desire the silver or the gold that is on them, nor take it unto thee, lest thou be snared therein: for it is an Abomination to The Lord thy God. Neither shalt thou bring an Abomination into thine house, lest thou be a cursed thing like it: But thou shalt utterly detest it, and thou shalt utterly abhor it; for it is a cursed thing".

Deuteronomy Chapter 13:17.

"And there shall cleave nought of the cursed thing to thine hand: that The Lord May Turn from The Fierceness of His Anger, and Shew thee mercy, and have Compassion upon thee, and multiply thee, as He hath Sworn unto thy fathers".

Judges Chapter 2:11-15.

"And the children of Israel did evil in The Sight of The Lord, and served Baalim: and they forsook The Lord God of their fathers, which brought them out of the land of Egypt, <u>and followed other gods, of the gods of the</u> <u>people that were round about them,</u> and bowed themselves unto them, and provoked The Lord to anger. And they forsook The Lord, and served Baal and Ashtaroth. And The Anger of The Lord Was Hot against Israel, and He Delivered them into the hands of the spoilers that spoiled them, and He Sold them into the hands of their enemies round about, so that they could not any longer stand before their enemies. Whithersoever they went out, The Hand of The Lord Was Against them for evil, as The Lord Had Said, and as The Lord Had Sworn unto them: and they were greatly distressed".

Whatever it is, and whoever it is that takes our Relationship away from The Characteristics of God's Spirit and Truth, then that Person, People, Nations, Cultures and Dominions, they are the other gods The Lord Is Asking is Chosen People to make certain that we do not practice what they are practicing to thus damage The True

Connection that we have Developed and is Maintaining for The True and Living God.

Don't be amazed about how quick it is that others can accumulate wealth and success for their lives, the devices that they are using, if it is outside of The Will of Almighty God, they will and must lose that which they have earned, because has it stands, these are the practices of the other gods.

Be in Relationship with your God and wait for your God to Move, because when God Moves and thus Manifest within the lives of His People, then that which God Has Done Will Remain Fixed for All Times and All Seasons, and nothing and no one can remove or take away that which God Has Given for His People to Inherit as long as we remain Faithful to The God of The Universe.

To The God of Unlimited Understanding, Knowledge and Wisdom, Jesus Christ The King of kings and The Lord of all lords, The One God Which Was, Which Is and Which Is to Come. From The Ministry of The Church of Jesus Christ Fellowship, Savannah Cross, Jamaica, West Indies. God Bless, from Pastor Lerone Dinnall.

Be Careful of The Other gods...

Just Meditate Until You Break Into Prayer...

Message # 105

Date Started January 19, 2019
Date Finalized January 19, 2019.

2 Kings Chapter 6:8-12.

"Then the king of Syria warred against Israel, and took counsel with his servants, saying, In such and such a place shall be my camp. And The Man of God sent unto the king of Israel, saying, Beware that thou pass not such a place; for thither the Syrians are come down. And the king of Israel sent to the place which the Man of God told him and warned him of, and saved himself there, not once nor twice. Therefore the heart of the king of Syria was sore troubled for this thing; and he called his servants, and said unto them, Will ye not shew me which of us is for the king of Israel? And one of his servants said, None, my lord, O king: but Elisha, the Prophet that is in Israel, telleth the king of Israel the words that thou speakest in thy bedchamber".

Hebrews Chapter 4:12.

"For The Word of God Is Quick, and Powerful, and Sharper than any twoedged sword, piercing even to the dividing asunder of soul and spirit, and of the joints and marrow, and is A Discerner of the thoughts and intents of the heart".

To The God that Revealeth Secrets, to The God of Always The Higher Level of Anointing, to Him Be All Glory, Honor and Praise. I am Privileged and Blessed to Be God's Anointed Vessel through whom Secrets Are Revealed. Here we go again, the time is now 3:24 AM of January 19, 2019. I Received A Vision of Subtil Attack towards My Life and that of My Family, while not understanding the Movement of the spirits action of Attack and where the Attack is coming from, I Heard The Voice of The Lord Said and Repeated this Word Three Times:

"Just Meditate Until You Break Into Prayer"...

The Lord Allowed me to Understand That because Iniquity is the Main Sin that is Identified by His Will to Erect Judgement on those who deserves to be Judge, The God Lead Couple and People of God have got to be very Careful of how they use words in Prayer, to send Words to those who are not necessarily their enemies, because every word that proceeds out of the mouth of A Child of God Has the Power to destroy, and if that which is sent is focused on those who are not responsible, then those who have offered the Prayer would have Manufactured upon their own heads the counter-attack of their own words falling upon their own lives.

The Lord Reveals that He Is A Just God, and He Stands as A Firm Protection for those who will walk in His Will, therefore The Lord Reveals to Me that A Child of God Has to Elevate to The

Continual Higher Level In God to therefore Identify Through The Operation of The Holy Ghost as to When an Attack is Coming and also to Be Sensitive to a Touch to Identify Where and Who the Attack is coming from, and this must be done carefully before Prayer is Made, because that Prayer of Warfare which is going to be made, is indeed The Sword of The Spirit of God, which will go forth to Execute that which The Word of The Spirit so desires to be Fulfilled.

Thus The Lord Revealed within The Vision that I Must Meditate for a while so that The Spirit Man Can Fully Understand Where, Who and What the Attack is, to therefore channel the Senses of The Spiritual Man to Direct the Prayer of The Sword to Where The Sword Must Be Sent.

The Lord Allowed me to Understand that The Children of God or Sons of God is so Effective in Prayer that when we allow for The Spirit Man's Full Attention to be acquired, the Simplest of Words spoken by The Spirit Man Destroys Mountains and Pull down False Altars, therefore, The Sons of God Need not to consider in a Prayer of warfare to be Lengthy, because if The Spirit's Full Attention is Acquired, then when we say Move, whatsoever is there has to Move; if we Say Dead Man or Dead Bodies, then members of False Altars must die, because it will not be the Voice of The House of Clay that is Talking, but it is realized that it is The Spirit Man that Dwells within the Temple of that house of Clay, therefore those Words that are spoken are not winds that Blows, but it is a Fact, those Words Represents The Same Voice that Spoke and Said:

"Let There Be Light"...

2 Kings Chapter 6:18.

"And when they came down to him, Elisha Prayed unto The Lord, and said, Smite this people,

I Pray Thee, with Blindness. And He Smote them with blindness according to the word of Elisha".

Don't worry, my job is not to Pray and ask God to Do Bad things to people, but this is My Prayer...

Father of Heaven and Earth, I come before You this day in The Name of Jesus Christ, Thou O God Art The God of Abraham, Isaac and Israel, Thou Art Also The God of Covenant, in that You Said, Those who Bless those who are under Covenant, You Will Bless them, and him that Curseth those who are under Covenant, You Will Curse Him. Father, I Pray that You Will Forgive me of all My Sins; Sins of the Past, Sins of The Present and also the Sins of The Future. Father, this is My Request after Meditating for a while before I Pray, and also in consideration towards Your Own Words upon my life and that which is Your Will Being Done, Lord I Pray that whatsoever a person have Imagined and have destined for my life and for the life of My Family and for The Ministry of The Church of Jesus Christ Fellowship, Lord I ask in The Name of Jesus Christ that, that which is their desires for others, may it be multiplied upon their own heads a hundred times fold.

To be Clear Lord, If Good is Imagined for Me, My Family and Your Ministry, then allow Good to be Multiplied an hundred times fold upon those who have Imagined and Purposed that for my life; and if it is that evil in whatever way is Imagined and purposed from any Persons, Altars, Witchcraft, Powers, Demonic practices; then In The Name of Jesus Christ, The God of Abraham,

Isaac and Israel, The God of Covenant, The God that Said I AM THAT I AM; The God that Said No Weapon that is formed against My People will never Prosper; The God that Said Upon this Rock I Will Build My Church and The Gates of Hell shall not Prevail against The Church; I Pray that as their desire is to destroy and to pull down that which God Has Set Up, let that which is the intent of their Minds to be recompensed upon their own heads and their family and their altars, an Hundred times in measurement, From The Spiritual to the physical and back to The Spiritual.

Lord I seek to remain in The Likeness of Your Will, this I Pray In The Almighty Name of Jesus Christ, Let Your Will Be Done on Earth as it is in Heaven, Amen.

Note: The Lord Revealed this important discipline to me a while back when I was Anointed by His Approval to become a Pastor to manifest an Altar for His Glory In The Name of Jesus Christ, this is the discipline that will affirm A Child of God's Relationship with their Father.

The Lord Speaks...

"Whatever happens within the lives of His Children that causes the direct interference of The Flow of The Spirit of God's Movement within a day for the life of any of His Children, that which has happened to A Child of God must be revealed to their Father before the Sun goes down, if it happens within the night period, then it must be revealed to their Father before the Sun has risen;

before revealing what took place to anyone, it must be revealed to The Father First".

A Child of God that has identified that after they have finished praying to their Father by revealing what took place within their circle that causes God's Spirit Flow to stop or be hindered, if this Child has followed this discipline which was Revealed by The Father to me, then because God Almighty is One God, the same result of the **ANSWER** that leads to the sure reaction from whom the forces of Iniquity has established from, the same **ANSWER** that leads to the reaction of God's Enemies will also be repeated again and again and again to signify The Authority of God that is manifested by simply A Child of God's Sincere God Instructed Discipline.

If This Discipline is followed by A Child of God, this Child of God will no doubt receive the same **ANSWER** that I always receive whenever I have made this prayer of Discipline unto My God that Instructed me to do it in this order before the Sun goes down and before the Sun has risen.

The **ANSWER** is This…

"Father Will Take Care Of It"…

The mention of The Title Father to A Child of God that is praying must bring forth the strongest approval within the Mind, Body and Soul, that whosoever, speaking of many, and whoever, speaking of one person, and wherever, speaking of evil altars; wherever these forces are coming from, it will not end well for them because The Highest Power Within The Authority Of God Declares and Decrees that He Will Take Care of It…

The Lord Instructed me to Reveal this important Discipline to His Children throughout the world. Remember that The Access Name Is Jesus Christ, not jesus or jesus's name but **JESUS CHRIST**.

161

I Hope that we were Educated by this Message to know how to treat situations in our lives that speak to different forces that would seek to Stop, Destroy or Prevent The Manifestation of The Glory of God over our Lives, and The Building of The Ministry of God within our Lives.

To The God of Continual Higher Levels, in The Name of Jesus Christ I Give Thanks. From The Ministry of The Church of Jesus Christ Fellowship, Savannah Cross, Jamaica, West Indies. Pastor Lerone Dinnall. God Bless.

Being Attacked By The Weapons Of The Enemy? What Should You Do In Accordance To God's Will? Just Meditate Until You Break Into Prayer...

Knowing How To Win The Game Of Chess Against The Enemy.

Message # 106

Date Started January 27, 2019
Date Finalized January 27, 2019

St John Chapter 10:6-10.

"This Parable Spake Jesus unto them: but they understood not what things they were which He Spake unto them. Then said Jesus unto them again, Verily, Verily, I Say unto you, I Am The Door of The Sheep. All that ever came before me are thieves and robbers: but the sheep did not Hear them. I Am The Door: By Me if any man enter in, he shall be Saved, and shall go in and out, and find pasture. The Thief cometh not, but for to steal, and to kill, and to destroy: I Am Come that they might have life, and that they might have it more abundantly".

I Give Honor to The Everlasting Father, King of kings and Lord of lords; Jesus Christ The Lamb of God. Again this is A Blessing to be found in this Position to Be The Replica of God's Mind. I was Given The Permission to use that Term Replica of God's Mind, therefore I'm Free.

The Lord Revealed to me that His People are being Humiliated because we've been Structured and Trained to fail before we've entered the Battlefield against The Enemy. Therefore, when it is seen that the Challenge of Oppression has arrived from Our Enemies, we find ourselves in a Position of being completely clueless of what we should do and the Position that we should hold to ensure that we are Victorious against every Challenge or Test the enemy has brought our pathway. We've been Taught Continuously how to keep silent and never to stand directly in front of our Enemies to show forth The Authority of The God that is inside of us.

Knowing God Is A Spirit of Confidence that Flows through our very Veins, it is expressed upon our very Features that we are not to be Messed with or Underestimated of what our True Potential is, which is Governed by The Ever Present, Unlimited Power of The Almighty God.

I've seen for myself the Fear in the eyes of God's People because of a Lack of meaningful Relationship with God. Fear that Causes even Anointed Mouths that once Prophesy The Will of God are placed on Mute, no longer having The Spiritual Anointing to speak and to Declare the words that Says:

"I Shall Not Die, But Live To Declare The Works Of The Lord".

We must learn that the enemy is Daring, meaning that the enemies of God's People operate by spirits that need and Must be fed to satisfy their dark spiritual growth. This means that the enemies will never stay at one level to attack the lives of God's People, but will always be growing with more and more spirits to satisfy the hunger of the dark authority.

It must now be observed from the lives of God's People that there must be Clean Spiritual Growth to now be able to counteract the levels of demonic forces that will seek to overcome The Anointing that is in the life of A Child of God.

There are some Christians that may be of the belief that when the enemy approaches A Child of God, their only duty is to observe and to wish us farewell on our walk with God. The Bible Seeks to Educate God's Children to be Born in the Understanding to Know that the enemy only approaches A Child of God with Three Intentions, which Is:

1. **To Steal What God Has Given for A Child of God to Possess.**
2. **To Kill, which Means by any means necessary, The Anointing that Governs our Lives must be stopped from Manifesting within Our Vessels.**
3. **To Destroy, this Means that when the enemy comes our way, his Intentions is not only to Destroy Husband and Wife, but Children which are the Continuation of that family must be wiped out as well.**

Therefore, it must be understood by every person that is living for God, that Our lives are Continual Targets for the enemy's weapon. We cannot afford to be confronted by the enemy and not find ourselves already in a Position where we are Trained to know how we need to Answer the enemy when they dare to speak to us.

I went to A Church recently, and was confronted with the spirit of fear within that Church; I was called to be the speaker and immediately The Anointing of The Lord Activated. And that which The Holy Ghost was demanding to Know is, what is it that the enemy has spoken that causes The People of God to be Fearful. Once this was identified, The Lord Allowed me to understand that He Has Given Me The Approval to Speak back to every Challenge or words of fear and discouragement that was spoken, to now cancel those words with The Anointed Words of God Which Says:

"I AM THAT I AM".

The People of God needs to Understand that if when the enemy speaks, if The Children of God remains in a Position of Being Mute, then that which the enemy has Declared over our lives must be Activated because there was no Anointing from us to Say:

"LET THERE BE LIGHT"...

I Encouraged The People of God by Reading A Scripture from The Book of 1 Samuel Chapter 17:45-47. Which State:

"Then said David to the Philistine, Thou comest to me with a sword, and with a spear, and with a shield: but I come to thee in The Name of The Lord of Hosts, The God of The Armies of Israel, whom thou hast defied. This day will The Lord Deliver thee into mine hand; and I will smite thee, and take thine head from thee; and will give the carcases of the host of the Philistines this day unto the fowls of the air, and to the wild beasts of the earth; that all the earth may know that there is a God in Israel. And all this assembly shall know that The Lord Saveth not with sword and spear: for the battle is The Lord's, and He Will Give you into our hands".

It must be noticed by God's People that David spoke three verses of Declaring What God Will Do for Him; he did not keep silent from the Horrible three verses that Goliath also spoke to him

166

before he spoke to Goliath. The words that Goliath spoke to David are as Follows:

1 Samuel Chapter 17:42-44.

"And when the Philistine looked about, and saw David, he disdained him: for he was but a youth, and ruddy, and of a fair countenance. And the Philistine said unto David, Am I a dog, that thou comest to me with staves?

And the Philistine cursed David by his gods. And the Philistine said to David, Come to me, and I will give thy flesh unto the fowls of the air, and to the beasts of the field".

My Readers will Identify that what David said to Goliath was in accordance to what Goliath declared that he was going to do to David. Can you just Imagine Goliath said all those words and David went **MUTE**. No Anointing to Declare and to Decree; No Authority; No God to Defend.

He would have been killed; because Goliath appearance would have been the spirit of dark forces that declared to David; and Goliath words would have been the decreed council of the Philistine's will of what should happen to David.

But because David Knew his Relationship with God, he Knew that The Authority of God Had No Equal. No Giant could stand before God then, therefore no gods can stand before The Authority of God within the life of A Child of God Now, nor will it be Possible for it to happen in the near or distant future. It Cannot Work! Because God's Authority Within A Vessel Will always spring forth Life in a dead condition. Greater is He that is in you, than he that is in the World.

I Encouraged The Saints that, if the enemy uses three minutes of words seeking to destroy A Child of God life, then The Child of God must also use three minutes of **WORD** to kill every spirits that has uttered destruction for the life of A Child of God.

Note: Every command the devil presented to Jesus Christ, for those commands God Revealed An Anointed Commandment that chased the devil away from The Presence of Jesus Christ. This must be Replicated from the Lives of God's People, that the enemies of God's People will know their Positions in this life which is to be under our feet and not in front of our Faces; because The Righteous Must Inherit The Earth.

The lesson in this Message is for God's People to Move according to The Wave of The Spirit of God, and The Wave of The Spirit of God Is Never the Aggressor, but rather, it is the Spirit of Patience that Tarries to See the movement of the enemy to thus counteract those movements with that which The Word of God Has Declared and Decreed, Tried and Tested for all times and can never Fail.

For every Child of God that has Mastered The Wave of The Spirit of God; these are the same Children of God that will become The Best Chess Player against the wiles of the enemy, that no matter what the enemy says or do, The Movement of A Child of God will be Far superior to that which the enemy has made.

In this Game of Chess with the enemy, we must understand that God Already knows the Play Book, therefore, nothing and no one surprises God.

Let us Abide in Relationship with God, that we can Understand The Movement of The Spirit of God. If God Is The Best, then We Are The Best, because we are His Children.

Remember to speak back to the enemy; open your mouth wide, and I Will Fill It.

This Message is A Spiritual Ammunition for God's People, therefore be ready to use The Spiritual Sword which is A Child of God Spiritual Mouth.

To The God of All Ages, Jesus Christ The Lamb of God. From The Ministry of The Church of Jesus Christ Fellowship, Savannah Cross, Jamaica, West Indies. Pastor Lerone Dinnall. God Bless.

Win The Game, Don't Just Play The Game!

Spiritual Transfer...

My People are destroyed for a lack of knowledge: because thou hast rejected knowledge, I will reject thee, that thou shalt be no priest to me: seeing thou hast forgotten the law of Thy God, I Will Also forget thy children. Hosea Chapter 4:6

Message # 108   **Date Started February 20, 2019**
Date Finalized February 25, 2019.

Genesis Chapter 2:15-17.

"And The Lord God Took the man, and Put him into the garden of Eden to dress it and to keep it. and The Lord God Commanded the man, Saying, Of every tree of the garden thou mayest freely eat: But of The tree of the knowledge of good and evil, thou shalt not eat of it: for in the day that thou eatest thereof thou shalt surely die".

Genesis Chapter 3:6-10.

"And when the woman saw that the tree was good for food, and that it was pleasant to the eyes, and a tree to be desired to make one wise, she took of the fruit thereof, and did eat, and gave also unto

her husband with her; and he did eat. And the eyes of them both were opened, and they knew that they were naked; and they sewed fig leaves together, and made themselves aprons. And they heard The Voice of The Lord God Walking in the garden in the cool of the day: and Adam and his wife hid themselves from The Presence of The Lord God amongst the trees of the garden. And The Lord God Called unto Adam, and Said unto him, Where art thou? And he said, I heard Thy Voice in the garden, and I was afraid, because I was naked; and I hid myself".

All Honor be unto The Lord our God, let God Be Exalted through The Name of Jesus Christ. It is an Honor to be in this position yet another time to Inspire God's People through words of Revelations from God.

I got this Topic based on the fact that The Spirit of God Lives inside My Vessel. The Lord Gave me clear Instructions when I was on the road, the date being February 19, 2019. I went somewhere and met someone who was interested in purchasing a used parts that I had available, upon letting that person know that the parts was available, therefore they can call me when they have decided their mind to purchase that which they needed, The Spirit of God Spoke through me and Said:

> **"You Don't need that person's money, because if you take that person's money their life that they are currently living will affect the life that you're living for Me".**

The person called me an hour after and told me that they needed the parts and had money to pay for the item. I remembered what The Lord Told me and gave the person an impossible price for the item, hence that person now said it was too expensive therefore they will seek the item from another source. I was relieved because I felt the Burning and I heard what The Voice of The Lord Spoke out of My Vessel concerning a person that I have never met before.

This event in my life brought back similar words that The Lord Spoke in the Past, which goes like this:

"The Purpose Of The Holy Ghost Is To Protect The Temple Of God".

Therefore whenever it is observed that A Child of God have entered an Atmosphere that will influence different spirits of which that person may not have the level of Authority that may be required to overcome that which they are now facing, The Spirit of God which is The Active Wall of Defence for that Child of God will now lift up a Standard that will Manifest that this Child of God will now be Protected by Warnings of Instructions to know what to do in order to overcome or to escape the rising Challenge that is fixed to cause interruption in the growth process of A Child of God.

The life of man entails everything that concerns that man, the clothes he wears speaks about that man, the food he eats, where he lives and where he works, those he associate himself with and even the Church that he attends or don't attend, the gifts he gives and most important, the money that he spends, all these different attributes of a man speaks about the life and spirit of that same man.

Now The Lord Revealed to me that A Child of God has to be extremely careful of who they would seek to receive Gifts or Money from, because the Foundation of that person which will manifest the type of life that such a person is living will now be given the permission by those who have received Gifts and Money from that person, the Ingredients of such a person's life will now circulate the type of spirit or spirits, demons and legions within the life of the person that have accepted that which comes from the person who is originally the giver of their life support.

How does this speak about the Topic Spiritual Transfer you may ask?

Seeking The Lord for the events that took place, The Lord Enabled me to understand a little deeper of what would have taken place if I had received that money coming from the life of a person that He Had Rejected to contribute of their life to my surroundings. This is what The Lord Said:

The Lord Speaks...

"Every Anointing and Authority that A Child of God Has Received from Him is a Fixed Blessing that God Has Released, however, that Anointing and Authority can be affected, based on the fact that this Spiritual Approval from God is not made fully effective. If that Child of God have not yet Mastered what is required to keep The Temple of The Lord Clean that these Spiritual Gifts can function in full capacity, then it will be realized that The Temple of God Is Restricted from Functioning. The Lord Reveals that if A Child of God have willfully granted access to someone of who their lives in the sight of God is to be compared to The Accursed thing, mainly spoken about in the Book of Deuteronomy and Joshua, if the Accursed things, which means a person's life which includes their Money and their Gifts, if this is made to dwell amongst that which is set aside for God's Use, then it would have cancelled the effects of The Anointing and Authority that such A Child of God have Received from God. That which was

Holy now becomes Unholy because of a lack of Spiritual Eyes to see what and who God Requires to be Entertained within the life of A Chosen Child of God".

I can just see the devil having his meetings of how he's going to inject different spirits in our circle based on the fact that we are not Knowledgeable of what Spiritual Transfer is. I speak the Truth, when The Lord Told me of this Topic, I never knew what it meant. It was the first I'm hearing of a term called Spiritual Transfer. The Lord then started to Educate me concerning a device that the devil has been using from the beginning of time, to thus steal the Anointing of

His Children who have not yet been Educated of what the devil is doing and what he has already done in the lives of many Believers.

The Lord Revealed to me that The Authority that He Had Appointed for Adam and Eve to carry out, that Authority was sneakily taken away through the counsel and channel of that which is called Spiritual Transfer. The Authority that Adam and Eve had, which was to have Dominion over God's Creation, was now transferred into the hands of the devil. This Authority was however retrieved by Jesus Christ when He died on The Cross for the fall of Adam and his descendants. Jesus Christ Said it is finished, Man's Redemption is Paid. He also said in The Book of Revelation Chapter 1:18.

"I Am He that Liveth, and was dead; and, behold, I Am Alive for evermore, Amen; and have the Keys of hell and of death".

This signifies The Authority that was transferred from man to the devil is now in the full Possession of Jesus Christ the Second Adam which Stands Firm forevermore for all those who would seek Salvation through His Name. This Authority no devil can steal again because it is wrapped up in Jesus Christ. But we can still be tricked by not being knowledgeable of what The devil is doing and how the devil is fulfilling his Mission to Delay The Authority in us, to cause God's Children not to have The Authority to Manifest as how we know we can Manifest for God.

It is observed in The Book of St Luke Chapter 4:1-13. This speaks about The Temptation that Jesus Christ Overcame from the Devil. It is seen that the devil was using the same method of Spiritual Transfer to again gain the Authority of not only man's dominion, but now he was seeking to capture The Authority of The Eternal God within the Vessel of Jesus Christ. And this is what The devil said:

1. **If Thou be The Son of God, Command this stone that it be made bread.**

2. **And the devil, taking him up into an high mountain, shewed unto him all the kingdoms of the world in a moment of time. And the devil said unto him, All this power will I give thee, and the glory of them;**
   Take A good look at what is said next.
   For that is <u>DELIVERED</u> unto me; and to whomsoever I will I give it.
   This statement from the devil will allow for us to understand that the Authority that he had was one that he received through the Subtil Sneaking Deception of how he caused Eve and Adam to spiritually sign the contract of Spiritual Transfer, without them even knowing what they had done.

3. **And he brought him to Jerusalem, and set him on a pinnacle of the temple, and said unto him, if thou be The Son of God, cast thyself down from hence: For it is written, He shall give his angels charge over thee, to keep thee: And in their hands they shall bear thee up, lest at any time thou dash thy foot against a stone.**

These three attempts from the devil was focused on how he could fulfill yet another Spiritual Transfer, the difference with this Transfer is that if Jesus Christ had **AGREED** to that which the devil had commanded, then it would have fulfilled the plans of the devil of that which he imagined in his mind when he was in heaven.

"I will build my kingdom above The Most High".

It is Important for My Readers to fully understand that in order for the devil to fulfill the clause and the condition of Spiritual Transfer, the devil needs the Free Will of the person of who he is seeking to Transfer Authority to first **AGREE** with that which he has now caused us to believe in, which means that the spiritual part of a man's life which is the Mind of a man have now Accepted. I'm often Teaching the members of The Church to never be in a rush to fulfill something that suddenly comes your direction and requires haste for it to be fulfilled. I'm not saying that The Lord at times will not Require us to do things in Haste, but this is different, because The Movement of The Lord Carries The Manifestations of The Lord. Therefore, if it is seen in your Relationship with God, that He Creates a Burning in your Body in a particular way, then it must be Identified at all times that The Resurrection of that same Burning Resembles The Movement of The Almighty God.

I need my Readers to take into consideration that all that the devil asked Jesus Christ to do He could have done it, He already had The Authority to Do God's Will; Take a note of that. The Authority to do God's Will but not man's Will or The devil's Will. But to do it at the request and command of the devil would have shown proof that The Son of God is Obeying the voice of the devil, thus The Authority that The Son of God Had would now become The Authority of The devil by just Agreeing with what the devil has commanded.

There are times we are challenged to do something that we know we have The Authority to Do, take for example laying Hands for someone to recover from a sickness or to Prophesy, these are Authority that The Lord Has Given for us to have dominion, but we must make certain that these Gifts with The Authority to Manifest is not being pulled out of us because we were pumped or commanded by other spirits and forces, but rather, we must always remember that we are continual Vessel for The Most High God, to Fulfill **ONLY** that which God Requires for us to fulfill.

The Response of Jesus Christ goes in this manner to the devil:

1. **It is <u>WRITTEN</u>, That man shall not live by bread alone, but by every word of God.**
2. **Get thee behind me, Satan: for it is <u>WRITTEN</u>, Thou shalt worship The Lord thy God, and Him only shalt thou serve.**
3. **It is <u>SAID</u>, Thou shalt not tempt The Lord thy God.**

I'm wondering if my Readers have Observed what was the Example The Lord Laid down for us to know how to answer the devil when Temptation does come?_____.

The Lord Reveals that A Child of God must always use The Word of God which forever Stands **FIRM** and nothing and no one can shake The Word of God that is **FIXED** in the life of A Child of God. The Word of God Stands Firm against all principalities and power, spirits, legions and demons, and it was proven again when the devil came to Tempt The Lord, that he could not stand in front of The Standard that The Word of God Has Manifested, he had to move.

The Lord Also Revealed to me that A Child of God in the process of Spiritual Transfer, if this Child God lean on The Wave of The Spirit of God, then it will be discovered through The Intelligence of The Most High God A Way to counterattack and overcome that which the devil is doing by implementing in that conversation a Sacrifice that is great, that even if the person that is seeking to get involved in your circle can fulfill that sacrifice, it would have cancelled the process of Spiritual Transfer because the master of the conversation is now in the power of The Child of God. Therefore, The Child of God is not Obeying the devil or the servants of the devil, but rather, the devil and the servants of the devil is now in agreement and obedience to The Voice of A Child of God. Authority and Anointing Remains upon and over that Child of God that is Wise to A Touch to Understand Spiritual Transfer.

The Lord Also Revealed that A Child of God has to open their Spiritual Senses to thus Remain Focused against those who are their fellow Brothers and Sisters, Pastors, Bishops, Ministers, Officers of The Lord or claimed to be Officers of The Lord. Spiritual Transfer is only attracted for those who have been Granted Special Authority from God for that Individual to **LOSE** that Authority. Therefore, A Child of God that is Anointed with Purpose from God has to walk with The Approval of The Wave of The Spirit of God because The Lord Has Revealed that it is a Fact, we **CAN** and will **LOSE** or Become Stifled from The Authority that God Has Freely Given to us. Prove for this Revelation can be found in The Book of 1 Kings Chapter 13. Verse 7-10.

> **"And the king said unto The Man of God, Come home with me, and refresh thyself, and I will give thee a reward. And The man of God said unto the king, if thou wilt give me half thine house, I will not go in with thee, neither will I eat bread nor drink water in this place: For so was it charged me by The Word of The Lord, Saying, Eat no bread, nor drink water, nor turn again by the same way that thou camest. So he went another way, and returned not by the way that he came to Bethel".**

It must be identified that the king, knowledgeable or not knowledgeable of Spiritual Transfer was without doubt seeking to fulfill the requirements that Spiritual Transfer could have been Activated within the life of this man of God. This was overcomed by the man of God because he was focused at that time to ensure that the Physical Manifestation of Attractions never trapped him to break the conditions of The Authority that he was to function under. This however was not the case in Verse 14-19. These verses must prove to A Child of God that we cannot only remain focused on those things that have the Physical Manifestation to deceive us, that will cause Spiritual Transfer to take effect within our lives. But we must now be Born in The Understanding and Knowledge to become Wise that our Spiritual Senses must always be at it ultimate best when it is that we are around Spiritual Manifestation, because has it was seen in The Scripture that the old prophet moved under the influence and spirit of being jealous of what the young prophet had accomplished in The Work of The Lord, thus having no care or respect for that which bind the young prophet to his contract of his Spiritual Authority with God. Transfer of Spiritual Authority was Activated upon the young prophet because he was now in Agreement by his own free will to Obey his new master that came in the Appearance of a old prophet, but it was in fact the councils of the devil devices to generate different challenges to be activated within the life of A Child of God. Spiritual Authority was broken from the life of the young prophet, this caused him to die because it was The Manifestation of The Authority from God that caused him to live and to go before kings and false prophets and still remain alive.

Bishop Austin Whitfield would often Teach The Church to let us Understand that the devil uses seven pens to write the different challenges that A Child of God must encounter, when one pen fails, then another pen is used to activate another challenge until all the pens are used.

Therefore, A Child of God must never think that the devil's action is conquered, but rather, we are given an absence from the trials for us to prepare for the greater challenge which is always coming. **Never Forget That!**

Can you just imagine how the devil is laughing at us, because we were not aware of what Spiritual Transfer Is! Every time in the past that The Lord Anointed us to fulfill certain task, we now discover that such Anointing was stolen by the devil, and people who are not Serving The Living God are now using The Authority that The Sons of God should be using because we are **IGNORANT** of Spiritual Transfer.

After this Revelation from God, I felt like if I had the power to go back in the past, I would punch myself in the face and say **WAKE UP!** Don't you see that the devil is tricking you!

Allow The Word of God to Stand Firm in us, while The Spirit of God is Made to Move in us.

Let Us Pray...

Father of Heaven and Earth, We give you all Glory, Honor and Praise from The Spiritual to the physical and back to The Spiritual. Father, we continually ask for Sins to be forgiven and for Iniquities to be Pardoned from the past, present and future. We Thank You through The Mighty Name of Jesus Christ that You Have Given Your People this opportunity that we are able to Pray and to give You Thanks that You Have Opened the eyes and senses of Your People, that we will become more and more Knowledgeable of the devices of the devil. Father we Thank You for Revealing Secrets, we Acknowledge that it's only through Your Divine Intelligence would we be able to gain Access to know of that which is in the council of the devil. We Pray Father of Heaven and Earth that

we will continue to be Obedient to Your Voice and The Movement of Your Spirit that we will always become an Overcomer of the enemy's trap. We Give You Thanks and Praise Continually through The Mighty Name of Jesus Christ, The Unlimited Mind of The Universe, Thank You, Amen.

All Glory, Honor and Praise Continually goes to Our Everlasting Father, The Prince of Peace, The God who is Alpha and Omega, The Beginning and the End, The God of all Mysteries and Secrets, In The Name of Jesus Christ, Thank You Lord. From The Ministry of The Church of Jesus Christ Fellowship, Savannah Cross, Jamaica, West Indies. Pastor Lerone Dinnall.

Be Careful Of Spiritual Transfer, You've Been Warned!

Write Your Personal Revelation From God, Add Your Special Touch To Your Book From This Ministry.

1. _____

2. _____

3. _____

4. _____

5. _____

6. _____

7. _____

8. _____

9. _____

10. _____

11. _____

13. _____

14. _____

15. _____

16. _____

17. _____

18. _____

19. _____

20. _____

21. _____

22. _____

23. _____

24. _____

25. _____

Closing Scriptures

1 Samuel Chapter 17:45-47.

"Then said David to the Philistine, Thou comest to me with a sword, and a spear, and with a shield: but I come to thee in The Name of The Lord of Hosts, The God of the Armies of Israel, whom thou hast defiled. This day will The Lord Deliver thee into mine hand; and I will smite thee, and take thine head from thee; and I will give the carcases of the host of the Philistines this day unto the fowls of the air, and to the wild beasts of the earth; that all the earth may know that there is A God in Israel. And all this assembly shall know that The Lord Saveth not with sword and spear: for the battle is The Lord's, and He Will Give you into our hands."

Ephesians Chapter 6:10-18.

"Finally, my brethren, be strong in The Lord, and in the power of His Might. Put on The Whole Armour of God, that ye may be able to stand against the wiles of the devil. For we wrestle not against flesh and blood, but against principalities, against powers, against the rulers of darkness of this world, against spiritual wickedness in high places. Wherefore take unto you The Whole Armour of God, that ye may be able to withstand in the evil day, and having done all, to stand. Stand therefore, having your Loins girt about with Truth, and having on the Breastplate of Righteousness; And your Feet shod with the preparation of the Gospel of Peace; Above all, taking the shield of Faith, wherewith ye shall be able to quench all the fiery darts of the wicked. And take the Helmet of Salvation, and The Sword of The Spirit, which is The Word of God: Praying always with all prayer and supplication in The Spirit, and watching thereunto with all perseverance and supplication for all saints."

Conclusion

Life teaches us this fact, that whenever an item has been overwhelmed, then that same item must reflect the birth of that which it was being filled with. All the brilliant minds in the world are seeking to find the answer of why things has just began to accelerate at a speed that cannot be explained, we look around and it looks like it's the same day that is observed for each morning, but the Spiritual Evidence speaks differently to suggest that the Sun of tomorrow is definitely not the same Sun that was experienced yesterday or even for today, the senses are just different, the heat is more observed and the time has become more vile. Everything is currently reacting differently because The Sovereign God Dictates that time is coming to its end to return back to where it was first Established, to The Unknown.

Sin is now pregnant, it is filled with the years of Iniquity which has been storing and now become full of its multiple desires, Sin is now in labour to bring forth even greater Abominations than that which is being experience on the earth presently, Sin is hungry to feed at all cost, this The Lord has Identified that His Time for the gathering of His People is Now.

> "Be Swift with My Words is what is Declared
> from The Mouth of The Almighty God; Those who
> will believe are those who are already preparing; Those
> who will not believe are those who have already made

their choice for the darkness of hell; Be Swift with My Words, Be Focused!"

The evidence of this Book will reveal that God is indeed Speaking to His People all over the World, and the preparation is one that is a personal walk, this Book is not Declaring for all people to be at a certain location or to give of all their money to support a cause, but rather this Book was Divinely Established from The Spiritual to reach those who are of The Spiritual and the Message is Clear as Day:

"Prepare Your Vessel To Be In Favor Of God's Movement Upon The Land"!

This Book is so important for believers that if your financially unable to purchase this Book and are truthful to the publishing firm that has published this Book, then it would be the instruction from myself and The Spirit God that some provisions will be made for the person that earnestly desires this Book, they will receive it to help amplify their path for God. If not by someone who will sponsor the purchase of this Book, then definitely through the channel of The Ministry that I am responsible for.

Armoured To Find The Light promises to raise the Spirit man within a Child of God that they too will become Spiritually Activated by The Father to go forth and become witnesses to those who need to experience The Light of God's Word for themselves. I'm often Teaching The People of God that if we can find ourselves redirecting our focus of God's Word to just one person at a time, then we would identify that the time that is spent on one person will blossom into Spiritual Fruits that will multiply in Heaven's Language.

This Ministry is not aimed to mislead God's People but to shine a brighter light for a Christian's own path of serving their Father in Spirit and in Truth. See for yourself within your personal relationship with God, and you'll identify for yourselves that the manifestation of God through your own relationship is pulling, pushing and burning your soul to identify that there is a different movement within The Spiritual, that is also manifesting a difference within the physical of this world. When a Child of God has experienced this fact for themselves, then you'll receive your own confirmation from your Father to Identify that it's time to look up.

God made this world to reflect balance, but when it is identified that balance has now become unbalanced then what will The Father Now Do? God's Final View is that of Kingdom Building, and God will never stand aside and watch darkness overflow and cripples the manifestation of the sure Inheritance that are marked by His Will to Establish His Final Kingdom, no, it will not work.

I hope and pray that those who have read this Book was blessed by The Divine Information that was furnished from this Book, again, as always, I will direct my readers to The True Source of Inspiration, The Lord of all lords and The King of all kings, The Saviour of mankind, Jesus Christ The Only Unlimited Mind of The Universe, to Him be All Glory, Honor and Praise, from Spirituality to Time Manifestation then back to Spirituality. From The Ministry of The Church of Jesus Christ Fellowship, Savannah Cross, Jamaica, West Indies. God Bless all His Children, From Pastor Lerone Dinnall.

www.ingramcontent.com/pod-product-compliance
Lightning Source LLC
Chambersburg PA
CBHW021626120626
46545CB00002B/425